WHAT WILL YOU DO IF

TRUMP

(OR HARRIS) WINS?

AN INTERACTIVE PICK-YOUR-PATH ADVENTURE

Second Edition. Published by Hyrax Publishing. © 2024 Daniel Hunter.
A work of speculative fiction — obviously. All rights reserved.
ISBN: 9798334719170; Independently published
All graphics by Elizabeth Beier.

YOUR JOURNEY BEGINS HERE...

Your friend calls while you are heading to your local polling place, exclaiming, "It's almost over!" It's been such a long campaign season.

You vote along with 160 million others. Then you await election results. You know counting will take many days — and that no matter the outcome, there will be accusations and denunciations.

IN THE END, WHO WINS?

Donald Trump wins, *turn to next page*
Kamala Harris wins, *turn to page 6*

On November 14th you're at home when you hear the results. After multiple counts and recounts, Donald Trump is announced president-elect of the United States. He won the Electoral College but once again lost the popular vote (by 5% to Kamala Harris).

You barely take a breath before your phone lights up with a notification: Donald Trump is delivering a fiery press conference. In his meandering way, he declares the election nearly stolen and claims he should have won the popular vote. He gains steam as he promises to lock up his political persecutors and "get justice" from the "corrupt courts." He closes to his cheering crowd, "We will wipe the woke mob off the face of the planet."

You sleep very poorly that night. Your mind races wondering which threats are just bluster and which he'll really try to enact.

DURING THE MONTHS BEFORE DONALD TRUMP TAKES OFFICE, WHAT DO YOU DO?

Join protests in the streets, *turn to page 8*
Connect with grassroots groups preparing for what's coming, *turn to page 9*
Wield legal and insider approaches to protect democracy, *turn to page 10*
Sit at home and weep, *turn to page 11*
Flee to Canada, *turn to page 12*
Create a small support team, *turn to page 13*

You're sitting at home idly wondering when the election will finally be over when an alert pops up on your phone: Kamala Harris has been elected. She won the Electoral College and the popular vote by a very narrow margin. The margins in three states are within 15,000 votes.

You scroll through the news wondering if Trump will concede. He does not. He puts on social media, "KAMALA IS ILLEGAL! I won by the bigggest margin ever! FIGHT TO SAVE OUR COUNTRY! STOP THE STEAL!" Days later, a few ballot-counting stations engaged in long-shot recounts are surrounded by angry mobs of Trump supporters. In Philadelphia and Madison, unexploded pipe bombs are found.

You watch things heat up. There are open calls for alternative electors to go to D.C. and cast their votes for Trump. As Vice President, Harris makes clear she will not seat any of Trump's fake electors. Large riots of Trump supporters break out sporadically around the state capitals of Pennsylvania, Michigan, and Nevada. Right-wing militias threaten to overtake state legislative buildings. Trump posts on social media: "January 6. Be wildER."

THERE IS A LULL DURING THE HOLIDAY SEASON. WHAT DO YOU DO?

Organize protests in the streets, *turn to page 14*
Train to be ready to take action if something happens, *turn to page 15*
Gather friends to prepare to defend each other, *turn to page 16*
Have quiet holidays and try to not think about it, *turn to page 17*

After Dwayne "The Rock" Johnson enters as a third-party candidate, all polling goes haywire. In an unexpected twist, the No Labels party put him on their ticket — joining with a half-dozen other minor parties. But it was a last-minute endorsement by "Stone Cold" Steve Austin that sent his favorability numbers skyrocketing.

Election results finally arrive on November 20. It was a nail-biter. It took three weeks to count the results. And then a bruising legal battle over the signatures — including getting the courts to recognize both "Dwayne Johnson" and "The Rock" as write-in votes for Johnson. He became the first write-in candidate ever to win the presidency.

President Johnson takes the mantle of president on January 20th. It is the largest audience ever to attend an inauguration. To the surprise of many, he goes on to institute a single-payer health care system, which saves the country billions. He uses those savings to lower the national debt. He ends U.S. poverty and creates world peace.

THE END

Well, you found the easter egg! No matter your dream, a third-party win is an excruciatingly unlikely scenario for this presidential cycle. Having a multi-party system is a good dream. Meanwhile, go back and explore options for the more likely scenarios.

Try again — or turn to Closing, page 156

You feel the need to signal widespread opposition, so you decide to join a January march in D.C. that promises to be a peaceful declaration that "we will not accept a dictatorship."

On the day of the march, the crowd around you carries various signs supporting abortion rights, calling for a pathway to citizenship for immigrants, promoting anti-fascism, and on and on. Though turnout is significant, fellow protestors whisper to each other that this march is much smaller than the Women's March in 2017.

As the crowd turns a corner, you see dozens of armed counter-protestors. With bats raised, they run at some of the marchers. You hear screams and see people pushing back, but you can't see exactly what is happening. When the police arrive, you watch the counter-protestors scurry away. They have gotten what they wanted — media reports of the march will mention violence.

Your friend texts you, worried if you're okay. "Trump has been on air all day calling your protest an insurrection." Trump repeats that he won "by a huge margin" and attacks the "small group of violent thugs trying to overturn the results of the election." He later says on social media that when he's president he'll order the military to clear the streets. You get home safe and sound and feeling energized by the march, but you wonder what it all achieved.

ON JANUARY 20TH, DONALD TRUMP IS SWORN IN AS PRESIDENT OF THE UNITED STATES.   WHAT DOES HE DO IN HIS FIRST 100 DAYS IN OFFICE?

Trump installs loyalists and opens IRS investigations into protest groups, *turn to page 18*

Trump talks big and issues 150 radical executive orders, *turn to page 19*

Trump talks big, but his chaotic office only completes ten major executive orders, *turn to page 20*

Trump invokes the Insurrection Act and orders the military into major Democratic cities, *turn to page 21*

You spend your time making a list of groups you are connected with who are ready to resist Trump's policies. You connect to national groups working on legal defense of the election, like Protect Democracy. You then turn to disobedience groups like The Disruption Project and ShutDownDC.

You call around to identify local groups and find a range of small, often under-resourced groups and nodes — like the local chapters of NAACP, Indivisible, and People's Action. You research training and scenario planning about what might happen and pass it around some of these local groups.

You remind groups what is coming. It will be chaotic. Many groups will be under attack. You tell people to stay calm. They are going to have to stick up for other groups — even when it doesn't affect them personally. And not just support each other on social media, but really bond and prepare.

Knowing others are out there who share your values, you feel better. You don't feel fully ready, but you feel better.

ON JANUARY 20TH, DONALD TRUMP IS SWORN IN AS PRESIDENT OF THE UNITED STATES.   WHAT DOES HE DO IN HIS FIRST 100 DAYS IN OFFICE?

Trump issues 150 radical executive orders, *turn to page 19*
Trump talks big, but his chaotic office only completes ten major executive orders, *turn to page 20*
Trump talks big but signs orders like a typical president, *turn to page 22*
Trump invokes the Insurrection Act and orders the military to the U.S.–Mexico border, *turn to page 23*

You find analysts and legal scholars who are preparing for what's coming. Some are downloading all the government's research on climate — convinced that, as he did in his first term, Trump will order all climate research to be scrubbed from the EPA, NASA, and other websites. Other groups prepare legal challenges, such as injunctions against the use of the military against civilians.

You end up joining a team writing a strategy for inside bureaucrats. The strategy is to urge them to not quit but to slow down the most destructive political orders. "Your oath is to the Constitution, not to a president."

It feels good to see the range of actors getting geared up. It's certainly a lot more than last time Trump was president. But inside your heart, you do worry it won't be enough.

ON JANUARY 20TH, DONALD TRUMP IS SWORN IN AS PRESIDENT OF THE UNITED STATES. WHAT DOES HE DO IN HIS FIRST 100 DAYS IN OFFICE?

Trump issues 150 radical executive orders, *turn to page 19*

Trump talks big, but his chaotic office only completes ten major executive orders, *turn to page 20*

Trump talks big but signs orders like a typical president, *turn to page 22*

Trump invokes the Insurrection Act and orders the military to U.S.–Mexico border, *turn to page 23*

You sense you should be doing something. But what can you do?

You sit at home and cry. You feel all the many, many things that have been lost. The many people whose lives are going to be severely disrupted — and lost.

As you flow deep into your feelings, you find it eases your mind to know that some things have already been lost — but other things haven't. The future remains largely unwritten. From ashes, beautiful things can grow. You aren't more hopeful, but you are more accepting and prepared to find out what you can do to help. You realize you have a false choice: either be engulfed in despair or focus on "self-care" that has you merely doing yoga. You pick neither — instead you choose to use the tears for healing and to engage with others in resistance.

ON JANUARY 20TH, DONALD TRUMP IS SWORN IN AS PRESIDENT OF THE UNITED STATES. WHAT DOES HE DO IN HIS FIRST 100 DAYS IN OFFICE?

Trump issues 150 radical executive orders, *turn to page 19*
Trump talks big, but his chaotic office only completes ten major executive orders, *turn to page 20*
Trump talks big but signs orders like a typical president, *turn to page 22*
Trump invokes the Insurrection Act and orders the military to U.S.–Mexico border, *turn to page 23*

You pack up your belongings and flee north to Toronto. For a while you ignore the news about the situation in your former homeland to the south. You invest yourself in Canadian politics. But you see how it is ugly, too. You're disgusted to learn the Canadian government is a major investor in an oil pipeline — despite claiming to have progressive climate policies. You watch how Donald Trump's anti-constitutional moves are echoed by autocratic wings inside Canada.

One day someone hands you a book about Jermain Loguen. He was a pastor who escaped slavery and established his home in Upstate New York. You read his words written after the Fugitive Slave Act passed. That law allowed white people to accuse any Black person, even one living in the North, of being a slave — and then incentivized judges with $5 more in pay if they sent the person into slavery.

Despite this, Jermain wrote, "We repudiate the idea of flight [to Canada] for these reasons; first that we have committed no crime against the law of the land, second resistance to tyrants is obedience to God, and third that liberty which is not worth defending here is not worth enjoying elsewhere." Courageously, he then published his name and address in the newspaper telling any fugitive slave that he'd help them along the Underground Railroad.

Meanwhile, President Trump rips apart the constitution. He forces the military to clamp down on pro-democracy protests. Democracy in Canada nose-dives, too, following in the footsteps of the bully to the south. With regret, you wish you had helped the Resistance. You live the rest of your life in Canada feeling deep remorse and wracking guilt.

THE END

The autocrat won this time. But you can try again. Sure, we know there is a history of people fleeing a country and playing a useful role in resistance from abroad. But for many people, it's a dream they clutch to support denial. Don't be in denial. You can do this. We can do this together.

Try again — or turn to Closing, page 156

You decide to adapt a process from Quakers called a "Clearness Committee." The idea is to listen deeply as people think through life choices to help them assess what their calling is in this moment. No advice — just listening. So you gather trusted friends and elders in your home.

Each person shares for about 15 minutes. It's going to be chaos. I'm so worried for my children. I don't want to do endless marches — we have to actually stop him. You can see people's tendency to self-protect — even though you believe that to make it, we'll have to stick our necks out for each other. Then people take turns asking questions to dig deeper: What are you willing to risk? What's important to you about doing that? Who do you need to be connected with? What do you need to carry that out?

You name your own and each other's skills and offerings. You have a gift for fundraising for causes. I really love talking to people in crisis. You sure are good at inspiring people to take bold action. You feel a little lighter and have some concrete options to consider. Knowing you have the backing of your community, you feel a little clearer.

ON JANUARY 20TH, DONALD TRUMP IS SWORN IN AS PRESIDENT OF THE UNITED STATES. WHAT DOES TRUMP DO IN HIS FIRST 100 DAYS IN OFFICE?

Trump issues 150 radical executive orders, *turn to page 19*

Trump talks big, but his chaotic office only completes ten major executive orders, *turn to page 20*

Trump invokes the Insurrection Act and orders the military into major Democratic cities, *turn to page 21*

Trump talks big but signs orders like a typical president, *turn to page 22*

It's hard to organize protests during the holiday season, but you do your best to put together some de-escalation trainings to address people's fears of counter-protestors.

The trainers walk people through a range of responses for different scenarios. Groups singing in formation can help deflect tension with counter-protestors. You can create a "flying squad" of highly trained people to form a barrier and fly into emergency situations. If violence does ensue, you see options ranging from calmly walking away in groups, to sitting down, to using physical means to protect your bodies. Choices mean power. You feel more powerful.

You pick a date and have your protest on a cold week in December. It's a decent turnout. In the end, 16 counter-protestors come and try to intimidate. But your group largely ignores them and drowns them out with songs. No violence happens.

BUT YOU ARE LEFT WONDERING, WHAT WILL HAPPEN ON JANUARY 6TH?

MAGA rallies at capitol buildings, *turn to page 24*
MAGA groups invade state capitals, *turn to page 25*
With Donald Trump at the lead, MAGA supporters again lead a violent attack on D.C., *turn to page 26*

You join people creating a Pledge of Resistance against a potential Trump coup. "If Trump does attempt a coup, we will take to the streets swiftly." The pledge goes viral and gets hundreds of thousands of signatures. You share the pledge with many of your friends, who are grateful to know there are options to express support for the election results.

You see a video of Stephen Zunes describing the four things regular people have done to stop coups successfully in other countries: widespread mobilization, building alliances, nonviolent discipline, and refusal to recognize illegitimate authority. You share this video with the pledgers.

You feel better and more prepared. You also now have a wider network of people you can connect with if something happens. You breathe a little easier.

STILL, YOU ARE LEFT WONDERING, WHAT WILL HAPPEN ON JANUARY 6TH?

MAGA rallies at capitol buildings, *turn to page 24*

MAGA groups invade state capitals, *turn to page 25*

With Donald Trump at the lead, MAGA supporters again lead a violent attack on D.C., *turn to page 26*

You worry about the political violence and about friends who may be targeted. You bring some of them together over dinner to talk about how you can support each other. Hearteningly, the conversation turns concrete, with discussion of setting up a secure message system on Signal for emergencies or sharing resources — like who has access to land or food if things go haywire.

You also share some grounded material about making repression and violence backfire. This country is awash with political threats, but most of that does not lead to actual political violence. You list behaviors that can help reduce real outcomes from the threats: having a public group of support, preparing for how to respond and reduce fear in worst-case scenarios, continuing to act boldly, organizing an emotional support team, and much more.

By the end of the evening, you feel satisfied and connected. You have a lot of people to follow up with. But you feel reassured knowing your neighbors and friends care about you.

STILL, YOU ARE LEFT WONDERING, WHAT WILL HAPPEN ON JANUARY 6TH?

MAGA rallies stay outside state and national capitals, *turn to page 24*

MAGA groups invade state capitals, *turn to page 25*

With Donald Trump at the lead, MAGA supporters again lead a violent attack on D.C., *turn to page 26*

You try your best to not think about what might happen. You try not to replay the violence of January 6, 2021. You try to forget that Trump may use every means available to get back into power. You try to ignore the wild things Trump has promised to do.

You are not successful. Your fear grows in the crevices of your mind. Rather than facing the reality of what people can do to resist Trump, the back of your brain just keeps sprouting new fears about what might happen.

You finally reach out to a trusted friend. They show you a resource called "What If Trump (or Harris) Wins?" It normalizes some of your fears, challenges others, and helps you to get a little more perspective. You feel a little more grounded. Just a little.

STILL, YOU ARE VERY SCARED. WHAT WILL HAPPEN ON JANUARY 6TH?

MAGA rallies at capitol buildings, *turn to page 24*
MAGA groups invade state capitals, *turn to page 25*
With Donald Trump at the lead, MAGA supporters again lead a violent attack on D.C., *turn to page 26*

Donald Trump's first day in office unleashes a blitz of executive orders. He closes the border with Mexico, a move immediately challenged (but not halted) in the courts. He withdraws from the Paris Agreement on climate change and orders the deletion of all climate research from government websites. He pardons himself and all the January 6th insurrectionists of all federal crimes. A week later he institutes a 16-week abortion ban, which is immediately frozen in the courts.

For the next 100 days, you tremble reading the news. Trump reclassifies 50,000 government workers as Schedule F employees so he can fire them all. The courts temporarily hold up this decision. But all cabinet members and political appointees are replaced by people screened for their loyalty to President Trump. Trump uses the Federal Vacancies Replacement Act to bypass the Senate and install hundreds of loyalists into his government.

Your friend notes the protests you were part of have become a Trump target. Trump's temporarily appointed head of IRS orders a freeze on the assets of the major organizations involved in the protest, calling it an "insurrection." The IRS opens an investigation into the nonprofit status of Planned Parenthood, MoveOn, and a dozen other organizations. Those organizations are told they may have their status revoked and assets frozen.

You realize you need to think more strategically. Protesting expresses opposition to Trump's policies, but it doesn't stop him from acting. You consider how you'd like to move in the upcoming months.

YOU ARE NOT PART OF ANY OF THE TARGETED GROUPS. WHAT DO YOU DO NOW?

Go back into the streets, this time armed, *turn to page 27*

Protect people who are being targeted, *turn to page 28*

Strategize acts of disobedience, *turn to page 29*

Start envisioning what happens after Trump leaves office, *turn to page 30*

Stay in reactive mode, responding only to the latest news, *turn to page 31*

Organize marches and public statements against Trump, *turn to page 33*

Defend existing institutions, *turn to page 34*

You're shocked by the speed at which Donald Trump moves. On his first day in office, he pardons himself and the January 6th insurrectionists of all federal crimes. He introduces a controversial executive order to reallocate government money toward building a wall on the U.S.-Mexico border, which is immediately challenged (but not halted) in the courts. He pulls out of the international climate change agreements (Paris Agreement) and stops all federal funding of climate adaptation, including halting NASA's and USAID's climate research. He reclassifies 50,000 government workers as Schedule F employees and tries to fire them, a move immediately halted by the courts — at least temporarily.

Day 2 keeps up the pace. Trump signs a "Back the Blue" order that extends legal protection for police and encourages them to arrest "people presumed as illegals." He orders ICE to prepare for mass deportations. The next week, right-wing militias set up checkpoints along the border with Mexico and begin terrorizing immigrant rights groups. Seemingly in support of the militias, at 2:34 am, Trump writes on social media, "ILLEGALS ARE DESTROYING AMERICA! SEND THEM BACK."

Lawsuits challenge many of the orders, including preserving almost two-thirds of those government jobs. Over the next 100 days, newspaper headlines are focused on keeping up with the massive changes. Trump uses the Federal Vacancy Replacement Act to bypass the Senate and install tens of thousands of loyalists into his government, including all cabinet and key positions. With his hastily assembled cabinet in place, he orders the Justice Department to investigate former U.S. Representative Liz Cheney and all of the House Select Committee on the January 6th Attack along with a list of 27 other "high-profile dissidents involved in stealing the election." His first 100 days feel like a blur.

YOU TAKE A BREATH. WHAT TO DO NOW?

Protect people who are being targeted, *turn to page 28*

Strategize acts of disobedience, *turn to page 29*

Start envisioning what happens after Trump leaves office, *turn to page 30*

Stay in reactive mode, responding only to the latest news, *turn to page 31*

Organize marches and public statements against Trump, *turn to page 33*

Defend existing institutions, *turn to page 34*

You can't help yourself. You end up watching Trump's first press conference. In front of hundreds of cameras, he invokes the Insurrection Action and orders the military to secure the border with Mexico. He announces plans for "the largest domestic deportation operation in American history." Later, you read a news article stating the order has already been challenged in court with rumors flying that some Trump advisors believe it was ineffectively written and won't hold up.

In the following days, he signs a few more executive orders. He pardons himself and all the January 6th insurrectionists of all federal crimes. He orders a halt to all government-led climate research and orders the U.S. to pull out of the international climate change agreements (Paris Agreement). He puts loyalists into his cabinet positions and attempts to use Schedule F to fire over 50,000 employees (a move immediately halted by the courts — at least temporarily). You keep hearing rumors of palace intrigue within the White House. You see though they are all loyal to Trump, his team remains ideologically diverse and bound mostly by shared grievances. The intrigue bursts into public when Trump fires several senior advisors at 3 am on social media: "THEYRE TRYING TO STOP MY AGENDA! ARREST ALL THE TRIATORS AND LOCK THEM UP."

Over the next 100 days, Trump's grievances outpace his orders — but even his grievances create real-world impacts. As court cases against him in Georgia continue, Trump posts a series of increasingly hostile messages, ending with the fiery, "BURN THE COURTS DOWN." The message is received by the Proud Boys and others who begin to harass Atlanta District Attorney Fani Willis at her home. Her home is firebombed twice. And her father, who was alone in the house, survives a drive-by shooting. Armed MAGA protestors intimidate court staffers across the country, calling them traitors.

YOU TAKE A BREATH. WHAT TO DO NOW?

Strategize acts of disobedience, *turn to page 29*
Start envisioning what happens after Trump leaves office, *turn to page 30*
Stay in reactive mode, responding only to the latest news, *turn to page 31*
Organize marches and public statements against Trump, *turn to page 33*
Defend existing institutions, *turn to page 34*

On his first day in office, Trump signs a series of executive orders. He reallocates government money toward building a wall along the border with Mexico. He orders a halt to all government-led climate research and orders the U.S. to pull out of the international climate change agreements (Paris Agreement). Trump reclassifies 100,000 government workers as Schedule F employees — making them "political" appointees that he can fire. Courts approve an injunction to all of this, but tens of thousands of government workers are now living precariously.

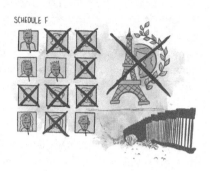

You end up watching his boldest move the next morning: At 10 am, Donald Trump invites cameras into the White House. You didn't mean to watch, but it was hard to peel your eyes away. He attacks the "lawlessness of Democratic cities" and promises to end it. He cites made-up crime statistics and the "wildly violent" protests since he's been elected. He invokes the Insurrection Act, ordering the military to go into Philadelphia, Los Angeles, Portland, and Chicago and "secure" them.

Your mind races as you keep scrolling through responses on social media. Several retired generals publicly decry the announcement as overly broad. The military operationalizes this objection through military courts, which order limited roles and a minimal use of force. The National Guard goes into the streets in the named cities but for now does little more than walk around. The fear of an explosion of violence is palpable. Democratic politicians scream this is an "abuse of power" — but refuse to use words like fascist or dictator on Trump's first week in office after winning a free and fair election.

YOU TAKE A BREATH. WHAT TO DO NOW?

Protect people who are being targeted, *turn to page 28*

Strategize acts of disobedience, *turn to page 29*

Start envisioning what happens after Trump leaves office, *turn to page 30*

Stay in reactive mode, responding only to the latest news, *turn to page 31*

Organize marches and public statements against Trump, *turn to page 33*

Defend existing institutions, *turn to page 34*

You can't help yourself. You end up watching Trump's first press conference. Trump emerges from the White House with a pen and Secret Service agents conspicuously by his side. In front of hundreds of cameras, he declares a state of emergency over the "influx of illegals at the Mexican border." He walks back into the White House.

This is far short of his campaign promise to "act like a dictator on day 1" and order the military to the border. But the authorization gives cover for others. Texas and Arizona governors order their National Guards to patrol the border extensively. Right-wing militias join the efforts, but most of Trump's base feels let down. To make up for it, he posts furiously through the night: "I AM YOUR JUSTICE. THIS IS JUST THE BEGINNING. Must purge the deep state."

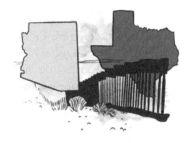

Over the next 100 days, Trump only signs a few more executive orders. He pardons himself of all federal crimes and all the January 6th insurrectionists. He pulls out of the Paris Agreement on climate change. He appoints loyalists in his cabinet. All these moves are the tamest versions of what some feared — but his base demands he do more, and faster.

Over the next 100 days, Trump's grievances outpace his orders — but even his grievances create real-world impacts. As court cases against him in Georgia continue, Trump posts a series of increasingly hostile messages, ending with the fiery-. The message is received by the Proud Boys and others who begin to harass Atlanta District Attorney Fani Willis at her home. Her home is firebombed twice. And her father, who was alone in the house, survives a drive-by shooting. Armed MAGA protestors intimidate court staffers across the country, calling them traitors.

YOU TAKE A BREATH. WHAT TO DO NOW?

Protect people who are being targeted, *turn to page 28*

Strategize noncooperation to remove Trump, *turn to page 29*

Start envisioning what happens after Trump leaves office, *turn to page 30*

Stay in reactive mode, responding only to the latest news, *turn to page 31*

Organize marches and public statements against Trump, *turn to page 33*

Defend existing institutions, *turn to page 34*

On his first day in office, Trump signs a series of executive orders. He reallocates government money toward building a wall along the border with Mexico. He calls a halt to all government-led climate research and orders the U.S. to pull out of the international climate change agreements (Paris Agreement). Trump reclassifies 100,000 government workers as Schedule F employees — making them "political" appointees that he can fire. Courts approve an injunction to all of this, but tens of thousands of government workers are now living precariously. Courts approve an injunction to all of this, but tens of thousands of government workers are now living precariously

You end up watching his boldest move that night, in time for the evening news: At 6:03 pm, Donald Trump invites cameras into the White House. He announces he's "finally ending the lawlessness on the border." He invokes the Insurrection Act, ordering the military to go to the border with Mexico and "shut it down." He announces plans for "the largest domestic deportation operation in American history."

You have trouble not constantly scrolling through responses on social media. As the actual text of the order leaks, pundits describe it as a generally lawful order to send the National Guard to patrol the hundreds of miles of unfenced border. The military's engagement is intended to be provocative, but military analysts suggest it does not intend to engage in any combat operations. Over the next 100 days, the border dominates news, with reports that fewer and fewer immigrants are crossing the border. Trump declares victory. Progressive Democratic politicians call the end-run around congressional authority an "abuse of power."

YOU TAKE A BREATH. WHAT TO DO NOW?

Protect people who are being targeted, *turn to page 28*
Strategize acts of disobedience, *turn to page 29*
Start envisioning what happens after Trump leaves office, *turn to page 30*
Stay in reactive mode, responding only to the latest news, *turn to page 31*
Organize marches and public statements against Trump, *turn to page 33*
Defend existing institutions, *turn to page 34*

MAGA militia hold rallies outside 35 state capitol buildings. For the most part, they do not attempt to go inside. Where they do (like in Harrisburg, Pennsylvania) they are met with minimal force from the police. The U.S. Capitol is heavily surrounded, with the National Guard already deployed. In D.C. there are no reports of significant violence.

But in the state capitol buildings, antifa groups show up to confront the MAGA supporters. Violent confrontations unfurl in a few cities. Three cities explode into raging violence during the nights, which actually grows as more people hear about it.

With the violence increasing, President Biden and President-Elect Harris jointly declare a state of emergency to deploy the National Guard. Perhaps sensing this, Trump posts: "We all know Lyin' Kamala stole this election. The military is with me! FREEDOM!"

YOU REALIZE THE NEXT FEW DAYS WILL MATTER A LOT IN HISTORY. WHAT DO YOU DO?

Join family-friendly street actions, *turn to page 36*
Go on offense by calling for reforms to the Insurrection Act, *turn to page 37*
Let the National Guard sort this out, *turn to page 38*
Move to protect targeted communities, *turn to page 39*

MAGA militia hold 35 rallies outside state capitol buildings. At first, they do not attempt to go inside. But then, angry and frustrated, they muscle their way past security. The media reports three deaths and generally calls it another "insurrection." Fox News hesitatingly calls it a "protest." Far right-wing news outlets like One America News Network call it a "liberation."

It's hard to tear yourself away from the news coverage on your phone. With their capitol buildings overrun, governors call for national backup. Biden invokes the Insurrection Act to remove MAGA protesters from the state capitol buildings. In some Republican-led states, MAGA protesters are greeted warmly by state legislators. MAGA protestors set up a long-term occupation of several capitol buildings, with demands that their state send Trump-supportive electors to certify the election — which would (illegally) swing the election to Trump.

Antifa groups show up at some capitol buildings and engage in violent confrontations with MAGA supporters. By the first night, eight state capitol buildings are still held hostage by MAGA groups. Donald Trump urges his supporters: "Free our country!"

YOU REALIZE THE NEXT FEW DAYS WILL MATTER A LOT IN HISTORY. WHAT DO YOU DO?

Join family-friendly street actions, *turn to page 36*
Call for broad reforms — an "Anti-Insurrection Act", *turn to page 37*
Let the National Guard sort this out, *turn to page 38*
Move to protect targeted communities, *turn to page 39*

26

Trump announces, "Heading to DC this weekend to take it back." MAGA militia leave the state capitals across the country to drive or fly into D.C. Fox News uncertainly calls it a "planned protest." Far right-wing news like One America News Network call it a "liberation." The intent of the Trump faction is clear.

President Biden, with Harris' support, invokes the Insurrection Act and mobilizes the military. D.C. becomes an armed fortress. In the days leading up to the protest, police arrest almost 1,000 Trump supporters on charges of illegal gun possession — a felony in D.C. You watch in horror on Saturday, as Donald Trump leads a march of over 50,000 people to the Capitol.

YOU REALIZE THE NEXT FEW DAYS WILL MATTER A LOT IN HISTORY. WHAT DO YOU DO?

Confront MAGA in the streets, *turn to page 40*
Join family-friendly street actions, *turn to page 41*
Call for broad reforms — an "Anti-Insurrection Act", *turn to page 42*
Let the military sort this out, *turn to page 43*

You know this is going to get ugly. You find others who are ready to go back into the streets for a march. You decide to attempt to shut down the IRS itself by physically blocking employees from getting in and out of the offices. You and other friends come armed, ready for violence.

As you expect, counter-protestors show up. They are heavily armed and aggressive. A wild street battle unfolds. Cops swarm and arrest dozens. It looks like some cops helped counter-protestors escape. You walk away with only a limp.

You're surprised that Donald Trump doesn't immediately say anything about it. Instead, Republican state governments publicly decry the actions. The head of the IRS accuses your group of terrorism. Liberal newspapers denounce the violence. Two leaders in your group are outed as FBI plants.

SO FAR, DONALD TRUMP HAS STAYED SILENT. WHAT DOES HE DO NEXT?

Trump ignores the protest and continues gaining control, *turn to page 44*
Trump orders the FBI to open investigations into the "domestic terrorists", *turn to page 45*

You watch as Trump's bombastic language fuels racist and bigoted actions. Hate crimes are up. Workplace violence is up. But under new leadership, Justice Department investigations are way down. In massive raids, people with brown skin or accents are swept up by ICE and summarily deported — often without meaningful access to thoroughly overburdened immigration lawyers. Health departments are losing funding and stretched beyond capacity. There are many, many needs.

You want to help, so you call a well-connected friend and arrange to meet her for coffee. She tells you of several efforts she knows about. "There are mutual aid groups popping up all over. Some are just online spreadsheets where people post needs and things they can offer. Others are very extensive, with full-time volunteers actively seeking resources within the community." She pauses to drink some coffee. "Because Trump has pulled government funding wherever he can — and even gone after nonprofit funding sources — there are some projects raising funds across multiple movement sectors as a kind of 'just in case' fund. People are motivated to give right now."

She then pauses and almost whispers the last, "And then there is the new Underground Railroad. It's a system of helping people find new homes in other states. Its work is mostly legal — but they help find new homes for people being doxxed by the right or for high-profile whistleblowers. Largely it's been helping undocumented folks find safe places to be — sometimes sanctuary cities, sometimes other places away from ICE."

YOU CONSIDER THOSE OPTIONS. WHICH DO YOU WANT TO SUPPORT?

Mutual aid society, *turn to page 46*
Joint emergency fundraising, *turn to page 47*
Underground Railroad, *turn to page 48*

You attend a training on civil resistance. "Most of us think that power flows downward from the president down to us low on the totem pole. But we need to think of power as flowing upward by our consent. If teachers don't teach, schools don't run. If people don't repair the roads, they become unusable. We describe this as the upside-down triangle model. Unjust authority on its own is naturally unstable and needs pillars of support to keep it upright — workers to keep the system chugging along so the powerful can keep their status."

The speaker goes on to quote Gene Sharp: "By themselves, rulers cannot collect taxes, enforce repressive laws and regulations, keep trains running on time, prepare national budgets, direct traffic, manage ports, print money, repair roads, keep markets supplied with food, make steel, build rockets, train the police and army, issue postage stamps or even milk a cow. People provide these services to the ruler through a variety of organizations and institutions. If people would stop providing these skills, the ruler could not rule."

Targeting pillars of support is a far more effective way of confronting authority than just marching in the street. "When you can remove a few pillars propping him up, just like Humpty Dumpty, he'll fall." That's how people power has been able to throw out dictators in the past.

YOU BEGIN TO THINK ABOUT DIFFERENT TACTICS TO BUILD PEOPLE POWER. WHAT DO YOU CHOOSE?

Create a widespread symbol of resistance, *turn to page 49*
Organize national strikes, *turn to page 50*
Support tax resistance, *turn to page 51*

You know it's not enough to simply be reactive to all the latest Trump announcements. Any prolonged effort at resistance will be unsuccessful if the movement is merely stuck in a defensive crouch. Prolonged defense is just another word for losing.

You decide to work on envisioning what happens after Trump leaves. You get ideas from a friend who is a cultural worker. You know she has written songs for movement organizations. But she explains that inside the resistance movement, many people are hurt and frayed. They need healing. And she thinks you could help bring some healing modalities and grounded spirituality to these spaces. You're not sure where that would take you, but you're curious.

Another friend says the problem is that we don't have a political vision of what's after Trump. "If the movement is going to disobey Trump's rules, we can't just tell people to ignore everything he says and does. We have to show what we stand for. When we get him out of office, we have to keep this kind of thing from happening again." Your friend is part of a political formation outside of the party system that's developing plans for a modern Constitutional Convention. This also sounds interesting.

YOU CONSIDER BOTH OPTIONS. WHICH ROUTE DO YOU PICK?

Provide cultural grounding for the movement, *turn to page 52*
Join the Constitutional Convention, *turn to page 54*

You wake up each morning and glance at your phone. You see the latest headlines written by editors who only get paid if you click: MAGA Doxxes Students, 1 dies. Trump Rips College Student Walkouts. Police Arrest Liz Cheney; Trump Vows "more vengeance." Mexico Border Explodes in Violence.

Each day you wake up worried what will happen next. You are horrified by the prospect of Trump returning for a third term. You post angrily on social media as Trump runs as a Vice President to Eric Trump — an obvious strategy to avoid prosecution and retain the power of the presidency. You post on social media and denounce friends who don't change their profile pic in support of the pro-democracy movement. But you can tell none of your actions are having an impact. Occasionally, you call up your cousin to argue. But mostly you watch with a growing sense of hopelessness that you spread to others.

During a long, late-night conversation, you bare your soul to your best friend. "There's so much bad news — I'm overwhelmed all the time. In my mind I get it. He is always doing new bad things, and we can't stop him by just playing defense. But I have trouble focusing on anything with so much bad happening." Your friend texts you an article about Finding Steady Ground. Its advice rings true, "When we're in bad shape, our power is diminished — we're less creative, more reactive, and less able to plan strategically. If we intend to stay active and effective in the world, we have a responsibility to tend to our spirits."

You start taking the seven practices in that article seriously — especially being conscious about "when and where I'll get news — and what I'll do afterward." By Trump's third term (officially as Vice President), you eventually join the movement and learn to be helpful. You teach others that the movement cannot win if it just responds to the latest bad actions of an autocrat. You wish you had been more grounded earlier.

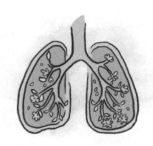

The autocrat won this time. But you can try again. Obviously, merely being reactive won't work. But it's attractive psychologically. Why? Because it reinforces the feeling that we have no agency — powerlessness can be an attractive drug. But there are lots of options — if only people would spend less time talking about what's wrong and more about what we can do to change it.

Try again — or turn to Closing, page 156

You rush into organizing marches — most with modest turnouts. You ask everyone you know which famous people they are connected with — and you try to get those celebrities to make public statements decrying Trump. One of your efforts takes off on social media and goes viral. Over several months of work, your effort gets major entertainment celebrities and Democratic politicians to denounce Trump as a "threat to democracy." With tens of thousands of likes and reshares, you feel good. But unease mounts.

The Trump train continues. He purges "disloyal" military leadership. He stops the Justice Department from investigating nearly all acts of racial bias and hate crimes. His Department of Education strips public education funding and pours it into private schools — before announcing plans to close the Department of Education itself. It's chaotic.

Marching felt empowering. But the bad news afterward makes some believe that nothing they do can make a difference. You happen to have a conversation with one of your smarter friends. She points out that you've been preaching to the choir without building power. "The left wing of this country has a lot of knee-jerk moves that serve primarily as identifiers without developing a lot of additional power. Marches are expressions of opinion — but they don't exert power, especially against an autocrat. He doesn't care…" You wonder if she's right.

AFTER PONDERING YOUR OPTIONS, WHAT DO YOU DO?

Go back into the streets, this time armed, *turn to page 27*

Protect people who are being targeted, *turn to page 28*

Strategize noncooperation to remove Trump, *turn to page 29*

Start envisioning what happens after Trump leaves office, *turn to page 30*

Stay in reactive mode, responding only to the latest news, *turn to page 31*

Go back into the streets, calling for even more people, *turn to page 35*

You watch Trump's moves threaten civic institutions. Trump's new Secretary of Education threatens to defund public schools. With an iron grip, Trump appoints young judges with extreme conservative views — reducing the courts' legitimacy. He constantly threatens, berates, and tries to intimidate the news media. You have trouble tracking all of the purges and appointments. You know these institutions are not perfect, but losing them entirely would be deeply destabilizing. And, especially at this stage, many of these civic institutions are keeping Trump's reign in check.

You decide to help defend those institutions you have some connections with. You know some military families, and the military is constantly under attack. Top generals are trying to hold the military together. Trump's orders present a huge problem for the military: Following his orders makes them look political, but not following his orders might break them in half. They're caught between a rock and a hard place. They're largely slow-walking orders and taking the middle ground. When Trump announced he was leaving NATO, they convinced him to do a "partial removal" that in practice will keep the U.S. active in NATO.

It seems wherever you turn he's gutted institutions. The EPA has been a chief target. He's ordered opening the Arctic National Wildlife Refuge for drilling for fossil fuels. Similar to the military, they're slow-walking those orders by sending them into a bureaucratic morass, further bogged down by their reduced staffing. You're aware that local wanna-be scientists, like yourself, could pick up some of the water and air testing that's getting missed — especially as Trump undid regulations to reduce coal pollution.

One night you hear poll worker friends talk about their challenges. Heading into the next elections, one of them faced a death threat — all have faced intense scrutiny and pressure in what are normally tame, quiet jobs. You think that's outrageous and can imagine doing more to defend election integrity — something you're deeply worried about.

WITH ALL YOUR INTERESTS, WHICH DIFFERENT INSTITUTIONS DO YOU TRY TO SUPPORT?

Organize veteran families, *turn to page 56*
Help the EPA as a citizen scientist, *turn to page 57*
Help protect the election, *turn to page 58*

A call is made for an even larger march. You initially jump in with enthusiasm. But it's a slog. Many of your friends say they're burned out by just marching without seeing changes. ("What's the point?") You know they're wrong that rallies don't matter. But you start getting clearer about when marches will benefit.

Marches are moments to show power. They show solidarity. They can inspire us. And in a vibrant democracy they can show passionate public opinion. But an autocrat doesn't care about public opinion, so that tactic won't work in isolation. You need more organizing to build power, nonsymbolic actions that shore up support against the dictator, and eventually direct confrontations in which large swathes of the population refuse to obey.

Just as you worried, the turnout for the march is half what it was last time. At first it's still great fun — beautiful signs, large banners, and upbeat music at the march itself. But with smaller numbers, it's a ripe target for right-wing counter-protestors. They swarm the march. Violence ensues. You get home safe, but a sinking feeling gnaws at you that other tactics might have been more effective.

Trump pounces. He decries the "violent WOKE mob" and invokes the Insurrection Act. Without people holding them accountable, military resistance to his orders collapses and the Army and National Guard begin coordinated raids to "put down protests" across the country. Sadly, others don't heed your call to do more than just march, like exploring rolling strikes. As Trump entrenches his power, the major tactics of resistance are dwindling marches by well-meaning rebels.

THE END

The autocrat won this time. But you can try again. This is probably the most controversial ending — because marching and protesting are extremely important! But Trump is good at using PR. And the tactics you chose didn't destabilize or challenge authority — they were just PR. Marches alone won't save us. We need to learn quickly to add other tools into our toolbox.

Try again — or turn to Closing, page 156

You organize your crew of people to head back into the streets. Though people are scared, you already showed them they can show up to face counter-protestors. This time it is not hard at all to find people willing to join you. Thousands join.

You have long arguments on the question of location. Eventually, people decide for tactical reasons that they will not directly engage the MAGA protestors. Instead, your aim is to contrast their behavior with yours. So you don't go directly to the Capitol, but instead go to a city square. You have a carnival-like atmosphere, with bubbles and street dancers. The images go viral.

When your protest is over, you have shown a family-friendly, pro-democracy event in contrast to the angry, armed insurrectionists. Some people from your protest go that evening to confront the MAGA protestors. But the story has been set in people's minds: The pro-democracy side is family friendly, while the anti-democracy side is violent and insurrectionist.

Biden and Harris order the National Guard to clear the state capitals. Trump explicitly urges the National Guard and police to "disobey Lyin' Kamala." He adds: "Lyin' Kamala's a thief. DON'T LET HER GET AWAY WITH STEALING YOUR COUNTRY!!!"

THE VIOLENCE CONTINUES IN THE STREETS. WHAT DO NATIONAL GUARD UNITS DO?

The National Guard obeys the chain of command, *turn to page 59*
The National Guard obeys Donald Trump, *turn to page 60*
The National Guard splits – some obeying Trump, others Biden/Harris, *turn to page 61*

You watch as Biden, Harris, and the military reassert control. The military wages a fierce internal battle to maintain unit discipline. You feel they'll succeed — Trump doesn't have enough levers of control. But you worry about the long-term cost and what happens after.

You find research from groups who have already articulated how we can combat extremism: reducing hate speech on social media, teaching a fuller understanding of U.S. history and its race- and gender-based violence, removing money from politics, changing the Electoral College, imposing greater penalties on people who undermine the election process, and so on. You join groups who are rallying around these changes as part of a wide-ranging bill proposed in the wake of recent threats to democracy.

When the riots are finally quieted on the street, the "Anti-Insurrection Act" is hard for even a reluctant Congress to avoid. Though the bill is watered down severely, major pieces are passed by Congress, shocked by the situation that has unfolded again.

The transition of power happens. On January 20, 2025, President Harris is inaugurated to fulfill a four-year term. The country weathers this tense period. You know there's much work ahead, but you feel proud for your role in helping your country avoid a coup and building an alternative.

THE END

You survived the transfer of power. But creating a deep democracy is a much bigger task ahead. Researcher Stephen Zunes has identified four things we need to stop a coup: widespread opposition, nonviolent discipline (to avoid giving the wanna-be autocrat excuses for more violence), alliance building, and refusal to recognize the coup plotters as legitimate.

Try again — or turn to Closing, page 156

Some of your friends are surprised you don't even join an action in the street. After all, the anti-coup research shows that widespread mobilizing of support is important — especially in keeping the military accountable for their behavior. But you feel like the National Guard can handle this.

As expected, Biden and Harris order the National Guard to retake the state capitol buildings. At first, they move quickly to clear out some of the Trump protestors and to quiet riots and unfolding street battles.

Trump keeps posting furiously on social media. During one night he posts 49 messages: "DON'T LET THEM STEAL AGAIN!" "I WON. THEY STEAL." "Our Great Country is Over if I don't become President."

THE NATIONAL GUARD SEES THESE MESSAGES. WHAT DO THEY DO?

The National Guard obeys Donald Trump, *turn to page 60*
The National Guard splits – some obey Trump, others Biden/Harris, *turn to page 62*
The National Guard obeys the chain of command, *turn to page 63*

While the street riots rage on, you think about folks who are being targeted by political violence outside of the media glare. Isolated, brave protestors in red, rural areas. Black and brown folks swept up in growing curfews. Immigrants being harassed by neighbors. You spend as much time as you can supporting them by helping them find basic needs, connecting them to advocacy groups, and supporting medics on the streets.

You watch as Biden, Harris, and the military reassert control. The military wages a fierce internal battle to maintain unit discipline. You feel they'll succeed — Trump doesn't have enough levers of control. But at what cost? Pro-democracy protesters play a critical role by showing widespread opposition. As best you can, you pick up the pieces in your community — lost wages, damaged buildings, scarred communities.

But the transition of power happens. On January 20, 2025, President Harris is inaugurated to fulfill a four-year term. The country weathers this tense period. Much of the mainstream media forgets that protestors were key in orchestrating this outcome. The military works to repair its image after internal divisions are exposed. You know there's much work ahead, but you feel proud for your role in helping your country avoid a coup.

THE END

You survived the transfer of power. But creating a deep democracy is a much bigger task ahead. Researcher Stephen Zunes has identified four things we need to stop a coup: widespread opposition, nonviolent discipline (to avoid giving the wanna-be autocrat excuses for more violence), alliance building, and refusal to recognize the coup plotters as legitimate.

Try again — or turn to Closing, page 156

You head to D.C. to confront MAGA face to face. You come prepared. But with D.C. in total lockdown, you can't get past the roadblocks. You fight with some MAGA supporters who also can't enter D.C. — but your vision of a grandiose intervention ends with a broken nose.

The violent clashes in D.C. peak. For a moment, it looks like a civil war could break out. But Donald Trump is not a general, and he doesn't have a clear internal team around him — just a lot of loyalists who bicker and fight. So when Trump is arrested on charges of treason, the Trump loyalists split into multiple, divided camps. They fight over tactics, strategy, location, and funding — and the military is able to regain control of D.C. Thousands of Trump supporters are arrested.

You begin to realize that without a clear strategy, you simply added to the chaos. The chaos became an opportunity for someone to be seen "cleaning it up" — it ended up being the military, but a smarter Trump could have tried to play that role. The lack of a widespread pro-democracy movement in that moment meant the military generals are now permanently seen as political forces, capable of deciding future elections. Anyone seeking the office of president now has to have secret meetings with military elites to seek their approval.

The transition of power happens on January 20, 2025 with a large military presence. President Harris is inaugurated to fulfill a four-year term. The country weathers this tense period, but barely. You know there's much work ahead, but you feel proud for your role in helping your country avoid a coup and building an alternative.

THE END

You survived the transfer of power, but you could have been more efficient. Researcher Stephen Zunes has identified four things we need to stop a coup: widespread opposition, nonviolent discipline (to avoid giving the wanna-be autocrat excuses for more violence), alliance building, and refusal to recognize the coup plotters as legitimate. In a coup situation, you don't confront the extreme — you speak to the middle.

Try again — or turn to Closing, page 156

You don't go to D.C. Instead, you organize local actions in a city square. You have a carnival-like atmosphere, with bubbles and street dancers. Your fears of counter-protestors don't materialize — the most extreme MAGA folks have largely gone to D.C. When your protest is over, you have shown a family-friendly, pro-democracy event in contrast to the angry, armed insurrectionists.

The violent clashes in D.C. peak. For a moment, it looks like a civil war could break out. But Donald Trump is not a general, and he doesn't have a clear internal team around him — just a lot of loyalists who bicker and fight. So when Trump is arrested on charges of treason, the Trump loyalists split into multiple, divided camps. They fight over tactics, strategy, location, and funding — and the military is able to regain control of D.C. Thousands of Trump supporters are arrested.

Your protests have had a reassuring effect. You later hear of a military colonel who says the protests helped shore up support inside the military. You certainly know it helped people around you feel less scared.

The transition of power happens on January 20, 2025 with a large military presence. President Harris is inaugurated to fulfill a four-year term. The country weathers this tense period, but barely. You know there's much work ahead, but you feel proud for your role in helping your country avoid a coup and building an alternative.

THE END

You survived the transfer of power. But creating a deep democracy is a much bigger task ahead. Researcher Stephen Zunes has identified four things we need to stop a coup: widespread opposition, nonviolent discipline (to avoid giving the wanna-be autocrat excuses for more violence), alliance building, and refusal to recognize the coup plotters as legitimate.

Try again — or turn to Closing, page 156

Groups have already articulated how we can combat extremism: reducing hate speech on social media, teaching a fuller understanding of U.S. history and its race- and gender-based violence, removing money from politics, changing the Electoral College, imposing greater penalties on people who undermine the election process, and so on. You join groups who are rallying around these changes as part of a wide-ranging bill proposed in the wake of recent threats to democracy.

The clashes in D.C. are violent. For a moment, it looks like a civil war could break out. But Donald Trump is not a general, and he doesn't have a clear internal team around him — just a lot of loyalists who bicker and fight. So when Trump is arrested on charges of treason, the Trump loyalists split into multiple, divided camps. They fight over tactics, strategy, location, and funding — and the military is able to regain control of D.C. Thousands of Trump supporters are arrested.

When the riots are finally quieted on the street, the "Anti-Insurrection Act" is hard for even a reluctant Congress to avoid. Though the bill is watered down severely, major pieces are passed by Congress, shocked by the situation that has unfolded again.

The transition of power happens on January 20, 2025 with a large military presence. President Harris is inaugurated to fulfill a four-year term. The country weathers this tense period, but barely. You know there's much work ahead, but you feel proud for your role in helping your country avoid a coup and building an alternative.

THE END

You survived the transfer of power. But creating a deep democracy is a much bigger task ahead. Researcher Stephen Zunes has identified four things we need to stop a coup: widespread opposition, nonviolent discipline (to avoid giving the wanna-be autocrat excuses for more violence), alliance building, and refusal to recognize the coup plotters as legitimate.

Try again — or turn to Closing, page 156

You don't do anything. You decide to just let this play out.

As you expect, the violent clashes in D.C. peak. For a moment, it looks like a civil war could break out. But Donald Trump is not a general, and he doesn't have a clear internal team around him — just a lot of loyalists who bicker and fight. So when Trump is arrested on charges of treason, the Trump loyalists split into multiple, divided camps. They fight over tactics, strategy, location, and funding — and the military is able to regain control of D.C. Thousands of Trump supporters are arrested.

You begin to realize that without a clear strategy, you simply added to the chaos. The chaos became an opportunity for someone to be seen "cleaning it up" — it ended up being the military, but a smarter Trump could have tried to play that role. The lack of a widespread pro-democracy movement in that moment meant the military generals are now permanently seen as political forces, capable of deciding future elections. Anyone seeking the office of president now has to have secret meetings with military elites to seek their approval.

The transition of power happens on January 20, 2025 with a large military presence. President Harris is inaugurated to fulfill a four-year term. The country weathers this tense period, but barely. You know there's much work ahead, but you feel proud for your role in helping your country avoid a coup and building an alternative.

THE END

You survived the transfer of power, but by leaning on the military instead of on people power. Researcher Stephen Zunes has identified four things we need to stop a coup: widespread opposition, nonviolent discipline (to avoid giving the wanna-be autocrat excuses for more violence), alliance building, and refusal to recognize the coup plotters as legitimate. In a coup situation, we need to be in the streets — and fast.

Try again — or turn to Closing, page 156

Donald Trump does what he's good at: changing the story. The courts denied his attempt to close the border outright. So he travels to the U.S.-Mexico border, calling it "the source of 80% of violence in this country." He creates a photo op of himself in body armor at the border.

The media's attention moves back to the border. Emboldened, Trump-inspired militias begin rounding up immigrants, sometimes in coordination with Immigration and Customs Enforcement (ICE). Violating all sorts of laws, these militias begin busing immigrants across the border into Mexico with relative impunity.

Meanwhile, Trump appointees replace government employees with loyalists. Inside, bureaucratic fights are commonplace. Trump loyalists make life excruciating for the remaining career civil servants; many institutionalists begin to trickle out. Controlling multiple levers of government, Trump installs judges across the country, freezes all legal cases against him, gerrymanders state election maps to ensure long-term Republican power, and announces that he plans to "stay in power until I can finish the job."

One night, you hear a knock on your door. It's the FBI. They have a warrant for your arrest on terrorism charges. You watch helplessly as they search your home.

LIBERAL GROUPS DISTANCE THEMSELVES FROM YOUR VIOLENCE. WHAT DO YOU DO NEXT?

Write from prison, *turn to page 64*
Give up — it's hopeless, *turn to page 65*

Donald Trump posts on social media that he's ordering the FBI to root out "domestic terrorists," including your group. At first, friends and relations call this an "overreach." Your hometown newspaper surprises you by opining that "it's illegal to order the FBI to target protestors exercising their 1st Amendment rights, even if they were armed." The sporadic efforts to resist this order matter — but you sense they don't extend beyond social media bubbles and, more importantly, that the movement doesn't develop more than symbolic actions.

The news cycle ebbs away from your case completely when the Supreme Court denies Trump's order to completely close the border. Like when he was denied the Muslim ban years ago, Trump adapts the order and tries again. Emboldened, Trump-inspired militias begin rounding up migrants, sometimes in coordination with ICE. Violating all sorts of laws, they begin busing them across the border with impunity.

Meanwhile, Trump appointees replace government employees with loyalists. Inside, bureaucratic fights are commonplace. Trump loyalists make life excruciating for the remaining career civil servants; many institutionalists begin to trickle out. Controlling multiple levers of government, Trump installs judges across the country, freezes all legal cases against him, gerrymanders state election maps to ensure long-term Republican power, and announces that he plans to "stay in power until I can finish the job."

One night, you hear a knock on your door. It's the FBI. They have a warrant for your arrest on terrorism charges. You watch helplessly as they search your home.

YOUR FRIENDS VISIT YOU IN JAIL TO BOOST YOUR SPIRITS. WHAT DO YOU DO NEXT?

Write from jail, *turn to page 64*
Give up — it's hopeless, *turn to page 65*

You look online to see if your neighborhood has any sort of mutual aid system set up. You don't find anything — so you post on Facebook and Nextdoor with a link to a simple spreadsheet where people can post needs and offerings. You list a few offerings and call some friends to add items to it. You get into the spirit, a contrast from the charity model of operating: "Everyone has something to offer, and everyone has things that they need."

It starts very slowly. Much of your time is spent cleaning up the spreadsheet. When nobody can meet a need, you research existing systems to point people to. The notes of appreciation do your heart good: a retiree who got help building their wheelchair ramp and then was able to offer piano lessons. Realizing food needs are a huge problem, you find some volunteers to help offer a once-a-week community meal. This brings a lot of attention to your work, but you still sense more could be done.

Your work speeds up rapidly when a local plant is raided by ICE. Apparently the owner called ICE on his undocumented workers right before payday. Workers flee en masse, uprooting their families. Suddenly your page is inundated with requests. And — thankfully — an almost equal number of offerings. The offers come from people from a wide political spectrum, and you carefully help people sort out care.

DESPITE YOUR HARD WORK, IT'S HARD TO NOT SCAN THE EYE-CATCHING HEADLINES:
NEWS ALERTS: *POLICE ARREST LIZ CHENEY,*
TRUMP ENFORCES COMSTOCK ACT, ICE SHOOTS THREE IN STANDOFF…

Ignore the news. Keep your head down — just do your work and stay small and nimble, *turn to page 66*

Get informed and read the news, *bookmark this page so you can return here and then turn to page 152*

AFTER YOU HAVE READ THE NEWS: YOU TURN FROM THE NEWS, YOUR COMMITMENT TO YOUR WORK REDOUBLED. WHAT DO YOU DECIDE TO DO NEXT?

Keep going, *turn to page 66*
Stay local, but expand your offerings, *turn to page 67*
Grow a national network, *turn to page 68*

You reach out to a few local nonprofits and funding circles. They all note how Trump's reduction in federal funding everywhere is squeezing them in turn. Bigger NGOs are largely making up for it with high-profile fundraising off anti-Trump sentiment, but very little flows to smaller groups. They are "surviving" but worry that further changes could prevent them from pursuing their missions.

You decide to try out a small joint fundraising venture. You bring a bunch of groups together for a fundraising event. All donations go to a local community funding source who channels them into the local groups. It starts very slowly — and you spend a lot more time than you expected answering details about who gets the money, when, and how. You build an extensive, open accountability structure — so the money is community directed.

A lot changes when a local plant is raided by ICE. Apparently the owner called ICE on his undocumented workers right before payday. Workers flee en masse, uprooting their families. Immigrant groups are struggling to find resources — right as their funding dries up. Your group is able to step up and deliver some needed money right away. The speed matters. People now understand what you're offering — and more offers come from people from a surprisingly wide political spectrum.

DESPITE YOUR HARD WORK, IT'S HARD TO NOT SCAN THE EYE-CATCHING HEADLINES:
NEWS ALERTS: *POLICE ARREST LIZ CHENEY, TRUMP ENFORCES COMSTOCK ACT, ICE SHOOTS THREE IN STANDOFF...*

Ignore the news. Keep your head down — just do your work and stay small and nimble, *turn to page 69*

Get informed and read the news, *bookmark this page so you can return here and then turn to page 152*

AFTER YOU HAVE READ THE NEWS: CLOSE THE NEWSPAPERS AND RETURN TO ORGANIZING THE EMERGENCY FUNDS. WHAT DO YOU DECIDE TO DO NEXT?

Keep going, *turn to page 69*
Stay local, but expand your offerings, *turn to page 70*
Grow a national network, *turn to page 71*

Your first act as an Underground Railroad "conductor" is when a community member who is undocumented reaches out. "I knew I needed to leave when my neighbor put all my contact information online," she said. "He'd already tried to call ICE on me at least three times. I need to get out of town."

The cases aren't numerous, but each requires operating with a mix of trust and secrecy. You become comfortable working on Signal, Jitsi, and other technologically secure products. Still, you are surprised how many of the "conductors" on the railroad are open about their work. But some need to be — that's the only way folks can find the railroad. And the part that's open allows the system verification that people are delivered to safe locations. Infiltration is a constant fear.

Your work speeds up rapidly when a local plant is raided by ICE. Apparently the owner called ICE on his undocumented workers right before payday. Workers flee en masse, uprooting their families. You team up with a bunch of others working on helping them find places to land — jobs, housing, and travel. You wish them all well, but (as is the rule) you don't have contact with them once they're on their way.

DESPITE YOUR HARD WORK, IT'S HARD TO NOT SCAN THE EYE-CATCHING HEADLINES:
NEWS ALERTS: *POLICE ARREST LIZ CHENEY,*
TRUMP ENFORCES COMSTOCK ACT, ICE SHOOTS THREE IN STANDOFF...

Ignore the news. Keep your head down – just do your work and stay small and nimble, *turn to page 72*

Get informed and read the news, *bookmark this page so you can return here and then turn to page 152*

AFTER YOU HAVE READ THE NEWS: YOU CLOSE THE NEWSPAPERS AND RETURN TO ORGANIZING THE UNDERGROUND RAILROAD. WHAT DO YOU DECIDE TO DO NEXT?

Keep going quietly, *turn to page 72*
Stay local, but go public, *turn to page 73*
Grow the national network, *turn to page 100*

When Denmark was occupied by Nazi Germany during World War II, the Danes created a simple symbol of resistance: wearing a paperclip on your shirt or coat. Given Trump's replacing so many bureaucrats — "paper pushers" — you feel this is a good symbol. Anyone can participate. The message is simple: "By wearing a paperclip, you agree to refuse to take orders, even push papers, for any autocrats. You only obey the Constitution."

You and many others spread the idea. Soon tens of thousands of people brand paperclips on their social media photos, wear them at work, and spread them all over the country. The symbol is a commitment "to refuse to do anything unconstitutional, anti-democratic." People sell rainbow-colored paperclips or U.S. flag-decorated paperclips. There's a pop song about paperclips that hits the charts. Among D.C. insiders, paperclips are secretly shown at personal risk.

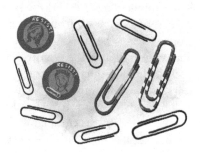

The New York Daily News begins to cover the protest, and soon commentators on CNN wear the paperclips just below U.S. flags. But the Trump train continues. Trump vows to arrest former U.S. Representative Liz Cheney and a dozen other "dissidents." Trump posts on social media: "IF YOUR PARENT IS WOKE, turn them in." His secretary of education orders a revamp of all school curricula to remove "woke references," which is widely understood to include references to the LGBTQ community and to slavery, like the 1619 curriculum.

THE PAPERCLIP MOVEMENT CHALLENGES TRUMP'S LEGITIMACY. WHAT DOES HE DO IN RESPONSE?

He ignores the protests and keeps consolidating power, *turn to page 74*

He publicly attacks the Paperclip Movement, *turn to page 76*

He orders arrests of leaders in the movement, *turn to page 78*

He orders the IRS to freeze assets immediately, *turn to page 80*

Organizing a strike is hard work, but people across the nation want to do something. The U.S. is so large that it's very hard to pull off a general strike. So organizers aim for a one-minute national strike. At 1 pm EST, all work is to be temporarily stopped for one minute. Doctors go on breaks. Transit halts across the country. Restaurants pause lunch service.

A one-minute "test run" of the strike is held in late 2025. When you walk around your downtown, few people seem to be striking. But when you watch videos from around the country of people, cars, and trucks halting in their tracks on the street, it does your heart good. You watch one bizarre video of traders on Wall Street who seem frozen in the middle of talking. At U.S. ports, bosses complain of lost income and threaten legal action against longshoremen for an unauthorized work slowdown. In a few small towns, businesses who join the protest are vandalized — but mostly, negative response to the strike is muted. It's a start.

Students at a few college campuses do impromptu walkouts, and workers from some local unions carry out wildcat strikes. But the strike organizers urge people to "keep their powder dry" and coordinate strikes for maximum impact. The threat to Trump is the growth of the movement. You are building power for large-scale national strikes around the country. Emboldened, the national strike organizers announce plans for a longer, 15-minute strike in 2 months time.

THE STRIKE CHALLENGES TRUMP'S LEGITIMACY. WHAT DOES HE DO IN RESPONSE?

Trump ignores the protests and keeps consolidating power, *turn to page 82*
Trump publicly attacks the strikers, *turn to page 84*
Trump orders arrests of leaders in the movement, *turn to page 86*
Trump orders the IRS to freeze assets immediately, *turn to page 88*

Supporting tax resistance makes sense: If Trump is going to use our tax dollars for oppressing our people, then we'll organize millions to stop paying their taxes. Even as you talk with others about it, you understand it's risky — and potentially costly with a threat of IRS fines. On the other hand, Trump's IRS is woefully underfunded and chaotically managed.

So you spend some time learning from groups like the War Resisters League and others who have done tax resistance as an act of conscience. You hear stories from people like Robin Harper, who documented every penny that he would have owed the IRS — but, as a lifelong Quaker and pacifist — refused to send his money to support war efforts. He never paid a penny or a fine since 1958. When the IRS knocked on his door, he welcomed them in and showed them his meticulous records of redirecting his money to good causes. Tax resistance may be purely symbolic — for example, reducing payment by $1 in protest. Or it might mean refusing to pay all taxes and instead donating that money to support positive causes like Robin did.

A campaign is launched that integrates all options. It starts with a simple promise, "If we get 10,000 people to join, we'll start meaningful tax resistance." Fueled by the awful moves of Trump, you get 10,000 signatories by the second week of the campaign. From there, it blossoms into nearly 100,000 people promising to withhold taxes. Some have already stopped paying estimated taxes.

THE TAX RESISTANCE CAMPAIGN IS CHALLENGING TRUMP'S LEGITIMACY. WHAT DOES HE DO IN RESPONSE?

He ignores the protests and keeps consolidating power, *turn to page 90*
He publicly attacks the Tax Resistance Movement, *turn to page 92*
He orders arrests of leaders in the movement, *turn to page 94*
He orders the IRS to freeze assets immediately, *turn to page 96*

You immerse yourself in the many different groups fighting Trump's policies. You spend time facilitating healing circles for the mutual aid community that's been supporting immigrants under attack. One strange night you get smuggled to an underground meeting with folks who are supporting a high-profile whistleblower high up in the Trump administration. She was outed and is feeling suicidal — you help connect her with resources to steady her.

It's deeply fulfilling work. And as you move around, you see the ways we are living in a culture of death. You see the community isolation and the frenetic pace. You see groups moving at the speed of light, often without a clear sense of purpose — just driven by a sense of need and reactive to the latest crisis.

You bring your spiritual gifts. You bring in musicians and body workers. You find poems and healing practices. You organize community events to help weave some of these different groups together. Oftentimes the different parts of the movement don't even know the other is out there — even though their missions overlap. You try your best to help ground the movement.

Over the next months, you see small political changes around you. But it feels like barely a dent amidst the national scene. Despite lower poll numbers, Trump continues filling the government with his loyalists. The courts eventually approve his Schedule F reclassification — 50,000 government workers are now being systematically replaced by Trump loyalists. Bureaucratic fights rage across many institutions. Trump installs judges across the country who gerrymander election maps in multiple states to give Republicans long-term power. But your heart tears as you see the language of fear and violence growing: immigrant communities terrified by right-wing militia patrols, increased violence against peaceful protestors, attacks on emissions standards, and exaggerated calls for political arrests.

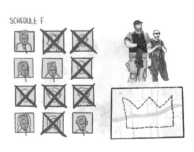

DESPITE YOUR HARD WORK, IT'S HARD TO NOT SCAN THE EYE-CATCHING HEADLINES:

NEWS ALERTS: *POLICE ARREST LIZ CHENEY,
TRUMP ENFORCES COMSTOCK ACT, ICE SHOOTS THREE IN STANDOFF…*

Ignore the headlines — keep doing your focused work, *turn to page 98*

Get informed and read the news, *bookmark this page so you can return here and then turn to page 152*

AFTER YOU HAVE READ THE NEWS: YOU TURN FROM THE NEWS, YOUR COMMITMENT TO YOUR WORK REDOUBLED. WHAT DO YOU DECIDE TO DO NEXT?

Continue your grounding work, *turn to page 98*

You arrive at your first meeting in Philadelphia. A group of national organizations have been meeting to discuss a "National Recommitment to the Constitution." They're clear that the convention has two parts. The first phase will be recommitting to the high values enshrined in the Constitution — such as free and fair elections. And the second phase will involve changes to the Constitution of "obvious things, like clarifying that corporations aren't people and money isn't speech." In the Trump era, these principles have never felt further away.

For a moment, you're worried it's all just talk. But one leader explains, "You know those government workers wearing paperclips? That movement is already using our language and guidance for their Constitutional Oath." The Constitutional Oath is a pledge to refuse any orders that undermine the Constitution, with an eight-point affirmation of the core principles.

The whole convention feels almost optimistic, starkly different from the toxic political environment. Despite lower poll numbers, Trump continues filling the government with his loyalists. The courts eventually approve his Schedule F reclassification — 50,000 government workers are now being systematically replaced by Trump loyalists. Bureaucratic fights rage across many institutions. Trump installs judges across the country who gerrymander election maps in multiple states to give Republicans long-term power.

These moves are discussed in the convention. In great detail, people lay out constitutional guardrails and explain how small reforms could ensure free and fair elections. It's easy to get lost in the weeds. But you make some strong relationships and find the people quirky and brilliant. Most intriguing, they plan a participatory process to "renew our sense of the Constitution." They envision tens of thousands of cities and towns across the country simultaneously deciding on key principles and values based on the Constitution. You're hooked. One of the leaders asks if you want to join their national leadership committee or build a local convention in your town.

DESPITE YOUR HARD WORK, IT'S HARD TO NOT SCAN THE EYE-CATCHING HEADLINES:
NEWS ALERTS: *POLICE ARREST LIZ CHENEY,*
TRUMP ENFORCES COMSTOCK ACT, ICE SHOOTS THREE IN STANDOFF…

Don't worry about the news — just organize a local convention, *turn to page 99*

Get informed and read the news, *bookmark this page so you can return here and then turn to page 152*

AFTER YOU HAVE READ THE NEWS: READING THE NEWS GIVES YOU A BETTER SENSE OF WHAT'S HAPPENING. YOU FEEL BETTER PREPARED.

Organize a local convention, *turn to page 99*
Grow the conventions nationally, *turn to page 101*

The situation with the military is dire. The strategy of slow-walking Trump's orders has an upper limit. Top generals consult with the Judge Advocate General's Corps over his most extreme orders and severely limit them based on the rules governing use of force. But a furious Trump forces some generals to resign and fires others. Frustrated, he replaces the chairman of the Joint Chiefs with a first lieutenant who is a Trump loyalist.

You talk with friends of friends who explain that the military establishment will resist becoming a political pawn, but it also won't disobey lawful orders outright. To do either would end the U.S. military as we know it. But worry has only increased. In the lower ranks there is more support for MAGA and frustration at the situation happening in the higher ranks. Some now worry about open revolt from below. Others worry that top generals won't be able to hold it together.

You begin reaching out to veterans and veteran family organizations — from the political left, right, and center — many of whom have deep connections with active duty military. You focus on families, reaffirming the oath of office and reminding the military that it is there to protect its entire citizenry. You sometimes couch this as avoiding the nearly unthinkable possibility that the U.S. military would actively fire on unarmed U.S. citizens. Other times you frame this as a fight for the military's survival — "It cannot survive being seen as politicized." And other times you help people recall themes from their training and codes of honor: The role of the military is to protect — not to score political points.

DESPITE YOUR HARD WORK, IT'S HARD TO NOT SCAN THE EYE-CATCHING HEADLINES:
NEWS ALERTS: *POLICE ARREST LIZ CHENEY,*
TRUMP ENFORCES COMSTOCK ACT, ICE SHOOTS THREE IN STANDOFF…

Ignore the news. Keep your head down – just do your work and stay small and nimble, *turn to page 109*

Get informed and read the news, *bookmark this page so you can return here and then turn to page 152*

AFTER YOU HAVE READ THE NEWS: YOU TURN FROM THE NEWS, YOUR COMMITMENT TO YOUR WORK REDOUBLED. WHAT DO YOU DECIDE TO DO NEXT?

Stay small, nimble, and quiet, *turn to page 109*
Become a larger, open group, *turn to page 110*

Like much of the government, staffing of the EPA has been gutted. The few of Trump's loyalists that went into the EPA to redirect the ship have faced stiff resistance. Buoyed by loosening regulations, companies are polluting more heavily — often flagrantly violating air and water safety standards. But the EPA does not have enough capacity to keep up all its research stations — or funding to fix those that break.

You map out some ways citizen scientists like yourself can help stretch the EPA's limited resources. You coordinate with universities to donate supplies and support student efforts. You are able to document real-time measurements of pollutants. The EPA can use them in court — and at least use them to track where to put their energy.

Your first readings of elevated results come in, with contaminants unique to a local coal-fired plant. You quietly report your results to the EPA. Your contact confirms these levels are hazardously high and likely illegal, even with Trump's more relaxed standards. These readings point to long-term health problems. Their enforcement wing comes in 3 months later and the coal plant pays a modest fine. It's a drop in a big bucket, but you know every bit helps.

DESPITE YOUR HARD WORK, IT'S HARD TO NOT SCAN THE EYE-CATCHING HEADLINES:
NEWS ALERTS: *POLICE ARREST LIZ CHENEY,*
TRUMP ENFORCES COMSTOCK ACT, ICE SHOOTS THREE IN STANDOFF…

Ignore the news. Keep your head down – just do your work and stay small and nimble, *turn to page 111*

Get informed and read the news, *bookmark this page so you can return here and then turn to page 152*

AFTER YOU HAVE READ THE NEWS: YOU TURN FROM THE NEWS, YOUR COMMITMENT TO YOUR WORK REDOUBLED. WHAT DO YOU DECIDE TO DO NEXT?

Stay small, nimble, and quiet, *turn to page 111*
Become a larger, open group, *turn to page 112*

You look ahead to the midterms and future elections, and you see much to worry about. The election infrastructure is under constant attack. Sure, even Trump-appointed judges keep tossing many of his challenges. But leaders in the "stop the steal" movement are now being appointed in federal positions to oversee the election. Most election infrastructure is local and state-based — and that's where you worry the most.

You connect with different efforts to safeguard the election. You read Protect Our Election's report, which asked election officials what they worried about and needed. They largely noted a lack of funding for their work — some states have even outlawed private funding while simultaneously reducing public funding. Most feel largely respected, but many report "inappropriate partisan pressure." You read about Washoe County, Nevada where three election directors resigned because of harassment.

You join with people who are doing local work and realize a practical way you can help: finding available grants. You don't know a ton, but apparently there are a bevy of local, state, federal, private, and other grants that election infrastructure can obtain. Nobody knows where they all go. The grants can help with digital security, voter education, training in cybersecurity, and hardening the election process. This feels like a way you can help out. You get your first $500 grant, and your election workers are overjoyed.

DESPITE YOUR HARD WORK, IT'S HARD TO NOT SCAN THE EYE-CATCHING HEADLINES:
NEWS ALERTS: *POLICE ARREST LIZ CHENEY,*
TRUMP ENFORCES COMSTOCK ACT, ICE SHOOTS THREE IN STANDOFF…

Ignore the news. Keep your head down – just do your work and stay small and nimble, *turn to page 113*

Get informed and read the news, *bookmark this page so you can return here and then turn to page 152*

AFTER YOU HAVE READ THE NEWS: YOU TURN FROM THE NEWS, YOUR COMMITMENT TO YOUR WORK REDOUBLED. WHAT DO YOU DECIDE TO DO NEXT?

Stay small, nimble, and quiet, *turn to page 113*
Become a larger, open group, *turn to page 114*

Many of the National Guard rank and file are Trump supporters. But military discipline takes precedence. In most cities, they carry out Biden and Harris' orders to quiet the riots. Over five tense nights, the National Guard uses hundreds of tear gas canisters and rubber bullets until the street fights quiet down.

Spurred by democracy protests, the FBI moves quickly to quell the uprising of MAGA supporters. In the following weeks, you watch as over 800 insurrectionists are arrested. Trump decries all this as a political witch hunt — but soon he, too, is arrested on charges of rebellion. For a time, the political anger in the country flares.

But the transition of power happens. On January 20, 2025, President Harris is inaugurated to fulfill a four-year term. The country weathers this tense period. Much of the mainstream media forgets that protestors were key in orchestrating this outcome. The military works to repair its image after internal divisions are exposed. You know there's much work ahead, but you feel proud for your role in helping your country avoid a coup.

THE END

You survived the transfer of power. But creating a deep democracy is a much bigger task ahead. Researcher Stephen Zunes has identified four things we need to stop a coup: widespread opposition, nonviolent discipline (to avoid giving the wanna-be autocrat excuses for more violence), alliance building, and refusal to recognize the coup plotters as legitimate.

Try again — or turn to Closing, page 156

For a moment it looks like the protests might quiet down. But two National Guard units announce their allegiance to Donald Trump. More follow suit. Many police units join, some officially and others unofficially. They make a public statement: "We will not let our elections be stolen again." They help MAGA protestors flood dozens of state capitol buildings.

Trying to stem the tide of revolt, Biden and Harris immediately invoke the Insurrection Act to end this "domestic insurrection." Under emergency powers, they freezes Donald Trump's social media company. The Justice Department opens an investigation. Military generals need to regain control. They order the Army to restrain the National Guard.

The next weeks are intense. You can sense the possibility of a full civil war brewing. Never-before-seen images of Army units versus National Guard units unfold on television screens. Tensions within the better-trained Army are minimal. Top military is intent on reinforcing unit discipline. Tension brews across the country. Reports grow of militias abducting immigrants with plans to "send them back across the border" and anti-Black and anti-Semitic attacks.

THINGS ARE TENSE EVERYWHERE. WHAT DO YOU DO NOW?

Confront MAGA directly in the streets, *turn to page 102*
Participate in a national strike, *turn to page 103*
Join family-friendly mass actions in public, *turn to page 104*
Let the Army do its job, *turn to page 105*

Most National Guard units obey the chain of command. But some do not — and where they don't, this causes widespread havoc. In Tallahassee, Austin, and Baton Rouge, the National Guard and city police open the doors to the state capitol buildings to welcome Trump supporters in. An anonymous joint statement is made explaining why they are countermanding orders, "We will not let our elections be stolen again." Pro-Trump protestors flood the capitols.

It is hard to tear yourself away from the news on your phone. Biden and Harris invoke the Insurrection Act to put down what they call a domestic insurrection. Army generals deploy troops to restrain the Nationall Guard units who were contemptuous of orders. Harris and Biden order Doanld Trump's social media company to be frozen, and the Justice Department opens an investigation into Trump supporting an insurrection.

The next weeks are intense. Never-before-seen images of army units versus National Guard units unfold on television screens. Tension brews across the country. Reports grow of militias abducting immigrants with plans to "send them back across the border" and anti-Black and anti-Semitic attacks.

WITH THE TENSION HOT, WHAT DO YOU DO NOW?

Confront MAGA directly in the streets, *turn to page 102*
Participate in a national strike, *turn to page 103*
Join family-friendly mass actions, *turn to page 104*
Let the Army do its job, *turn to page 105*

Many of the National Guard rank and file are Trump supporters. But military discipline takes precedence. In most cities they carry out Biden and Harris' order to quiet the riots. The few high-profile cases of rogue National Guard units go viral. But the military establishment clamps down and purges any internal resistance to taking orders. Over five tense nights, National Guard use hundreds of tear gas canisters and rubber bullets until the street fights quiet down.

Spurred by democracy protests, the FBI moves quickly to quell the uprising of MAGA supporters. In the following weeks, you watch as over 800 insurrectionists are arrested. Trump decries all this as a political witch hunt — but soon he, too, is arrested on charges of rebellion. For a time, the political anger in the country flares.

But the transition of power happens. On January 20, 2025, President Harris is inaugurated to fulfill a four-year term. The country weathers this tense period. Much of the mainstream media forgets that protestors were key in orchestrating this outcome. The military works to repair its image after internal divisions are exposed. You know there's much work ahead and hope you will play a more active role in the future.

THE END

You survived the transfer of power, but by leaning on the military instead of on people power. Researcher Stephen Zunes has identified four things we need to stop a coup: widespread opposition, nonviolent discipline (to avoid giving the wanna-be autocrat excuses for more violence), alliance building, and refusal to recognize the coup plotters as legitimate. In a coup situation, we need to be in the streets — and fast.

Try again — or turn to Closing, page 156

Many of the National Guard rank and file are Trump supporters. But military discipline takes precedence. In most cities, they carry out Biden and Harris' order to quiet the riots.

You realize the lack of an active movement resisting Trump has created long-term problems. The National Guard is seen by the right as a purely political force, capable of deciding future elections. People openly ask permission from the military before certain kinds of political protesting. You wish people had gone into the street — in any way — so it didn't seem like the National Guard was acting unilaterally.

But the transition of power happens. On January 20, 2025, President Harris is inaugurated to fulfill a four-year term. The country weathers this tense period. Much of the mainstream media forgets that protestors were key in orchestrating this outcome. The military works to repair its image after internal divisions are exposed. You know there's much work ahead, but you feel proud for your role in helping your country avoid a coup.

THE END

You survived the transfer of power, but by leaning on the military instead of on people power. Researcher Stephen Zunes has identified four things we need to stop a coup: widespread opposition, nonviolent discipline (to avoid giving the wanna-be autocrat excuses for more violence), alliance building, and refusal to recognize the coup plotters as legitimate. In a coup situation, we need to be in the streets — and fast.

Try again — or turn to Closing, page 156

You write scathing letters about dictatorships and the need to rebel against them. At first you are angry at groups who did not come out to defend you. You feel violently angry — which spikes when a Trump-appointed judge finds you guilty on terrorism charges and sentences you to 15 years in prison.

You spend the quiet hours in prison discussing and reading about how you got here. You learn about movements to fight dictatorships like those in Serbia. Dictator Slobodan Milošević incited his opposition into violence, knowing it would legitimize his crackdown. Once, he organized his supporters to protest on the same day and at the same location as opposition protests — with 20,000 police surrounding them. He understood that the more he could be seen as the force of "stability" against the violent hordes, the more stable his position would be. And it worked — until the opposition movement decisively chose a strategy that used internal discipline to refuse him those kinds of opportunities. They used humor, a decentralized structure, and poking fun at the dictator — not street confrontations — to gain widespread credibility and eventually remove him from power.

You realize a fight against a dictator is a fight over who has the broadest legitimacy in the public eye. Donald Trump was able to use a prolonged "state of emergency" to stay in power — despite the Supreme Court ruling against him — because he had gained too much legitimacy. You hope when you get released from prison you'll be able to teach the movement to be more strategic and sensitive to which tactics will win over a wider audience.

THE END

The autocrat won this time. But you can try again. An autocrat thrives in the domain of violence — because it gives them an excuse to stay in power. Their strongman image is often bolstered by chaos on the streets, which is why they work so hard to foment it.

Try again — or turn to Closing, page 156

You collapse in jail and feel the futility of changing such big systems. You eat very little. You grow pretty numb. You barely feel anything when the Trump-appointed judge finds you guilty on terrorism charges and sentences you to 15 years in prison. The first year of prison is tough. Your friends' visits do nothing to cheer you up.

You spend the quiet hours in prison discussing and reading about how you got here. You learn about movements to fight dictatorships like those in Serbia. Dictator Slobodan Milošević incited his opposition into violence, knowing it would legitimize his crackdown. Once, he organized his supporters to protest on the same day and at the same location as opposition protests — with 20,000 police surrounding them. He understood that the more he could be seen as the force of "stability" against the violent hordes, the more stable his position would be. And it worked — until the opposition movement decisively chose a strategy that used internal discipline to refuse him those kinds of opportunities. They used humor, a decentralized structure, and poking fun at the dictator — not street confrontations — to gain widespread credibility and eventually remove him from power.

You realize a fight against a dictator is a fight for the broadest legitimacy. You realize Donald Trump was able to use a prolonged "state of emergency" to stay in power — despite the Supreme Court ruling against him — because he had gained too much legitimacy. You hope when you get released from prison you'll be able to teach the movement to be more strategic and able to sense which tactics will win over a wider audience.

THE END

The autocrat won this time. But you can try again. An autocrat thrives in the domain of violence — because it gives them an excuse to stay in power. Their strongman image is often bolstered by chaos on the streets, which is why they work so hard to foment it.

Try again — or turn to Closing, page 156

You decide it's best to stay small. This allows you to prioritize your work locally. Plus, you see many friends burning out by constantly "doing more" to halt the ongoing Trump pronouncements. You resist that tendency. You do your part, but you feel your abilities stretched to their limits.

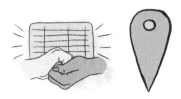

Food scarcity in your region haunts you. After a local plant was closed down, more people are turning to you for food needs. When a climate-change-fueled fire burns through town, you reach your breaking point. You struggle mightily to find resources — housing, furniture, food…

Over the next year, you see small political changes around you. But it feels like barely a dent amidst the national scene. Despite lower poll numbers, Trump continues filling the government with his loyalists. The courts eventually approve his Schedule F reclassification — 50,000 government workers are now being systematically replaced by Trump loyalists. Bureaucratic fights rage across many institutions. Trump installs judges across the country who gerrymander election maps in multiple states to give Republicans long-term power. But your heart tears as you see the language of fear and violence growing: immigrant communities terrified by right-wing militia patrols, increased violence against peaceful protestors, attacks on emissions standards, and exaggerated calls for political arrests.

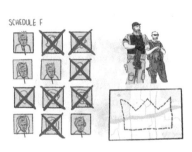

YOU ARE WALKING HOME WHEN A FRIEND TEXTS URGENTLY.

Read the text message, *turn to page 117*

Food scarcity in your region haunts you. After the plant was closed down, more people are turning to you for food needs. When a climate change-fueled fire burns through town, you reach your breaking point. True to the mutual aid model, you emphasize it's not about charity — it's about people getting what they need and offering what they can.

You decide to adapt your strategy a bit. You keep the community meal going, but add opportunities over meals for people to talk about why the system is the way it is. "Needing things is not a personal failure — we are living in a profoundly unequal society without safety nets." People begin connecting their personal struggles to larger politics, like Trump's cuts in government programs or climate change. You affirm this among your volunteers and during meals. You lose two volunteers who feel you are being anti-Trump. But others join in and offer to help develop new programs: community tree planting and meet-ups at retirement homes to avoid isolation. The volunteers talk about the benefits of trees for reducing asthma and climate change.

Over the next year, you see small political changes around you. But it feels like barely a dent amidst the national scene. Despite lower poll numbers, Trump continues filling the government with his loyalists. The courts eventually approve his Schedule F reclassification — 50,000 government workers are now being systematically replaced by Trump loyalists. Bureaucratic fights rage across many institutions. Trump installs judges across the country who gerrymander election maps in multiple states to give Republicans long-term power. But your heart tears as you see the language of fear and violence growing: immigrant communities terrified by right-wing militia patrols, increased violence against peaceful protestors, attacks on emissions standards, and exaggerated calls for political arrests.

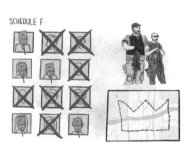

YOU ARE WALKING HOME WHEN A FRIEND TEXTS URGENTLY.

Read the text message, *turn to page 117*

You connect with other mutual aid groups across the country. Each is set up in a different way — some with extremely flat hierarchies and some even with semi-paid staff. You don't want to change how they operate, but you begin networking them to see their interconnections and help the nation see how mutual aid is holding together the fabric of society.

You launch a national Mutual Aid Network. Like when your local plant closes, people share needs and offerings and step up quickly. Sometimes it morphs into a climate and disaster relief service, almost like a decentralized, community-resourced Red Cross. When your community gets hit by climate change-fueled fires, you are able to raise funds nationally to ship community-sourced materials that the local community helps distribute. When the Mississippi River floods dozens of berms, you network with local mutual aid groups. You explain in one national interview, "We're showing that people can help other people. It's by mutuality that we evolve and grow — not by division."

Over the next year, you see small political changes around you. But it feels like barely a dent amidst the national scene. Despite lower poll numbers, Trump continues filling the government with his loyalists. The courts eventually approve his Schedule F reclassification — 50,000 government workers are now being systematically replaced by Trump loyalists. Bureaucratic fights rage across many institutions. Trump installs judges across the country who gerrymander election maps in multiple states to give Republicans long-term power. But your heart tears as you see the language of fear and violence growing: immigrant communities terrified by right-wing militia patrols, increased violence against peaceful protestors, attacks on emissions standards, and exaggerated calls for political arrests.

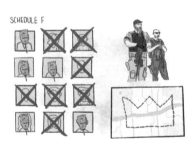

YOU ARE WALKING HOME WHEN A FRIEND TEXTS URGENTLY.

Read the text message, *turn to page 117*

You decide it's best to stay small. This allows you to prioritize your work locally. Plus, you see many friends burning out by constantly "doing more" to halt the ongoing Trump pronouncements. You resist that tendency. You do your part and feel good about it.

Even still, your part feels huge — especially as crises mount. A climate-change-fueled fire rages through town. A right-wing militia march ends up burning local businesses. Your funds are constantly depleted, and you're barely able to keep up with the need. But the work you're doing is good — and while you wish you had more resources, nobody else is stepping in at the speed that your group is. Without much to lose, you decide to be more explicit about your funding politics and announce a new fundraising challenge. For every right-wing marcher last week, you'll raise $100 to donate to local progressive causes. Two members of your funding circle quit in protest, feeling it's too anti-Trump. But you raise twice that amount by the end of the next day.

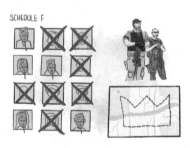

Over the next year, you see small political changes around you. But it feels like barely a dent amidst the national scene. Despite lower poll numbers, Trump continues filling the government with his loyalists. The courts eventually approve his Schedule F reclassification — 50,000 government workers are now being systematically replaced by Trump loyalists. Bureaucratic fights rage across many institutions. Trump installs judges across the country who gerrymander election maps in multiple states to give Republicans long-term power. But your heart tears as you see the language of fear and violence growing: immigrant communities terrified by right-wing militia patrols, increased violence against peaceful protestors, attacks on emissions standards, and exaggerated calls for political arrests.

YOU ARE WALKING HOME WHEN A FRIEND TEXTS URGENTLY.

Read the text message, *turn to page 116*

Your local work leaves you with so much to do. A climate-change-fueled fire rages through town. Your funds are constantly depleted, and you're barely able to keep up with needs. None of the established funding sources can move as fast as you can. You wish you had more resources — so you scheme an ambitious plan.

When a right-wing militia march ends up burning local businesses, you take two steps. You deliver no-interest loans to local businesses to repair their shops — before the city even sends them a loan application. But you also write an op-ed for the newspaper: "As a community resource, we cannot quietly stand by. Marches to scare and intimidate are wrong. Members of our community belong." You announce a challenge — for every right-wing marcher, you'll raise $100 to donate to local progressive causes. Two members of your funding circle quit in protest. But you raise twice that amount by the end of the next day.

Over the next year, you see small political changes around you. But it feels like barely a dent amidst the national scene. Despite lower poll numbers, Trump continues filling the government with his loyalists. The courts eventually approve his Schedule F reclassification — 50,000 government workers are now being systematically replaced by Trump loyalists. Bureaucratic fights rage across many institutions. Trump installs judges across the country who gerrymander election maps in multiple states to give Republicans long-term power. But your heart tears as you see the language of fear and violence growing: immigrant communities terrified by right-wing militia patrols, increased violence against peaceful protestors, attacks on emissions standards, and exaggerated calls for political arrests.

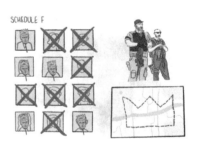

YOU ARE WALKING HOME WHEN A FRIEND TEXTS URGENTLY.

Read the text message, *turn to page 116*

While your local nonprofits are being (barely) propped up, there are serious fundraising droughts across the nation — especially at the hyper-local level. You decide to step in and ambitiously set up a national organization. It's surprisingly easy to capitalize on funding opportunities when Trump does outrageous things — like announce he's going to dismantle the EPA. (He doesn't, but it doesn't stop you from using the threat for fundraising.)

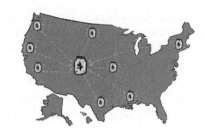

The real challenge is figuring out how to be a national regranting body to local groups. You do your best to vet local groups and to create an accountability structure that people can see — but you sacrifice speed for precision. You decide to abandon the model of month-long or year-long granting processes and move at lightning speed. This leads to mistakes and some money is poorly used. But, in the chaos of the times, your work is understood and generally appreciated. It means you can move fast. When climate-change-fueled fires burn through your town and when right-wing militia burn down Black businesses, you are able to move fast and decisively.

Over the next year, you see small political changes around you. But it feels like barely a dent amidst the national scene. Despite lower poll numbers, Trump continues filling the government with his loyalists. The courts eventually approve his Schedule F reclassification — 50,000 government workers are now being systematically replaced by Trump loyalists. Bureaucratic fights rage across many institutions. Trump installs judges across the country who gerrymander election maps in multiple states to give Republicans long-term power. But your heart tears as you see the language of fear and violence growing: immigrant communities terrified by right-wing militia patrols, increased violence against peaceful protestors, attacks on emissions standards, and exaggerated calls for political arrests.

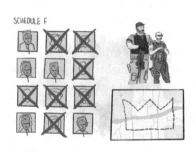

YOU ARE WALKING HOME WHEN A FRIEND TEXTS URGENTLY.

Read the text message, *turn to page 116*

You decide it's best to stay small and not talk openly about your work. Being quiet allows you to have some intimate conversations you might miss if you are more open. Plus, you see many friends burning out by constantly "doing more" to halt the ongoing Trump pronouncements. You resist that tendency. You do your small part and feel good about it.

There is plenty to do with crises mounting. After a local militia burns Black businesses, you help a local businessman who had a bomb placed in his car and believes he's the primary target. Each case is a lot of work and painful — nobody wants to be uprooted from their home. But many people don't have the resources to go to a new place. One high-profile case tests you — a relatively high-ranked EPA whistleblower releases a trove of confidential and unflattering documents about the inner chaos and bureaucratic fights of Trump's presidency. She is fired and repeatedly doxxed after being outed by a confidant.

That work feels meaningful. But it does feel small. Your work feels like barely a dent amidst the national scene. Despite lower poll numbers, Trump continues filling the government with his loyalists. The courts eventually approve his Schedule F reclassification — 50,000 government workers are now being systematically replaced by Trump loyalists. Bureaucratic fights rage across many institutions. Trump installs judges across the country who gerrymander election maps in multiple states to give Republicans long-term power. But your heart tears as you see the language of fear and violence growing: immigrant communities terrified by right-wing militia patrols, increased violence against peaceful protestors, attacks on emissions standards, and exaggerated calls for political arrests.

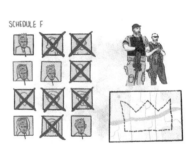

SCHEDULE F

YOU ARE WALKING HOME WHEN A FRIEND TEXTS URGENTLY.

Read the text message, *turn to page 115*

There is plenty to do with crises mounting. After a local militia burns Black businesses, you help a local businessman who had a bomb placed in his car and believes he's the primary target. Each case is a lot of work and painful — nobody wants to be uprooted from their home. But many people don't have the resources to go to a new place. One high-profile case tests you — a relatively high-ranked EPA whistleblower releases a trove of confidential and unflattering documents about the inner chaos and bureaucratic fights of Trump's presidency. She is fired and repeatedly doxxed after being outed by a confidant.

At this point, you decide to go public. You're inspired by a conductor on the original Underground Railroad named Jermain Loguen. He was a fugitive slave. Even after the Fugitive Slave Act was passed (which meant anyone could accuse him of being a slave and send him back south), he printed his address in the Syracuse, New York newspapers and told any fugitive slave they could come to him for help. You like that kind of openness. While some of today's conductors choose to be that open, many have remained anonymous for fear of harassment. You decide to risk the consequences. You pen an op-ed to the local newspaper about the general nature of your work, keeping all the appropriate things secret. Within days, more work comes your way.

That work feels meaningful. But it does feel small. Your work feels like barely a dent amidst the national scene. Despite lower poll numbers, Trump continues filling the government with his loyalists. The courts eventually approve his Schedule F reclassification — 50,000 government workers are now being systematically replaced by Trump loyalists. Bureaucratic fights rage across many institutions. Trump installs judges across the country who gerrymander election maps in multiple states to give Republicans long-term power. But your heart tears as you see the language of fear and violence growing: immigrant communities terrified by right-wing militia patrols, increased violence against peaceful protestors, attacks on emissions standards, and exaggerated calls for political arrests.

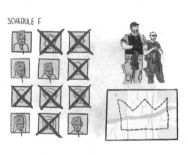

YOU ARE WALKING HOME WHEN A FRIEND TEXTS URGENTLY.

Read the text message, *turn to page 115*

Donald Trump ignores the protest movement. The Supreme Court allows him to proceed with firing 50,000 government workers under Schedule F. He fills the government with loyalists. Bureaucratic fights take place everywhere. Trump loyalists make life excruciating for institutionalists who remain, forcing resignations and further purgings. With control of multiple levers of government, Trump installs judges across the country who gerrymander election maps in multiple states to give Republicans long-term power.

It's not all loss. Trump floats a bill outlawing abortion after 16 weeks. The protest movement galvanizes direct actions all over the country. "Hands off my body." Congress halts the bill. Analysts point to Trump's decreasing approval ratings in the polls. And the courts hand Trump another setback when they rule, for the second time, against his bill to close the border with Mexico. As a result, the military again withdraws from policing the border.

But Trump doubles down on everything. He vows to return the military to the border. Emboldened right-wing militias echo ICE's mass deportation plans with frightful scenes of armed men strolling through immigrant neighborhoods. Trump opens up the Arctic National Wildlife Refuge to drilling. He vows to "introduce an abortion bill that everyone will love."

The resistance wing is uncertain. You know you cannot do reactionary protests to everything he does — much less proposes. But many criticize the movement as too ineffective. The Paperclip Movement has hundreds of thousands of participants, at various levels. Some want to escalate by announcing the movement will make certain we have open and fair elections — on the bet Trump might prevent this. You wonder if you need a bigger perspective to see who is out there and where to find more energy.

DESPITE YOUR HARD WORK, IT'S HARD TO NOT SCAN THE EYE-CATCHING HEADLINES:
NEWS ALERTS: *POLICE ARREST LIZ CHENEY, TRUMP ENFORCES COMSTOCK ACT, ICE SHOOTS THREE IN STANDOFF...*

Ignore the news. No time — just keep doing what you're doing, *turn to page 108*

Get informed and read the news, *bookmark this page so you can return here and then turn to page 152*

AFTER YOU HAVE READ THE NEWS: YOU TURN FROM THE NEWS, YOUR COMMITMENT TO YOUR WORK REDOUBLED. WHAT DO YOU DECIDE TO DO NEXT?

Stay the course with the allies you have, *turn to page 108*
Organize a large gathering with new partners, *turn to page 127*

Frustrated by reports of his falling approval ratings, Trump tests several lines of attack. "THEY ARE THE PAPERLESS MOVEMENT." When news of the shaky economy emerges, he turns back to your actions, "Their minds are CLIPPED." He calls it the "Bent-backwards movement." You wonder if his mind is slowing down.

The Supreme Court allows him to proceed with firing 50,000 government workers under Schedule F. He fills the government with loyalists. Bureaucratic fights take place everywhere. Trump loyalists make life excruciating for institutionalists who remain, forcing resignations and further purgings. With control of multiple levers of government, Trump installs judges across the country who gerrymander election maps in multiple states to give Republicans long-term power.

It's not all loss. Trump floats a bill outlawing abortion after 16 weeks. The protest movement galvanizes direct actions all over the country. "Hands off my body." Congress halts the bill. Analysts point to Trump's decreasing approval ratings in the polls. And the courts hand Trump another setback when they rule, for the second time, against his bill to close the border with Mexico. As a result, the military again withdraws from policing the border.

The resistance wing is uncertain. You know you cannot do reactionary protests to everything he does — much less proposes. But many criticize the movement as too ineffective. The Paperclip Movement has hundreds of thousands of participants, at various levels. Some want to escalate by announcing the movement will make certain we have open and fair elections — on the bet Trump might prevent this. You wonder if you need a bigger perspective to see who is out there and where to find more energy.

DESPITE YOUR HARD WORK, IT'S HARD TO NOT SCAN THE EYE-CATCHING HEADLINES:
NEWS ALERTS: *POLICE ARREST LIZ CHENEY,*
TRUMP ENFORCES COMSTOCK ACT, ICE SHOOTS THREE IN STANDOFF…

Ignore the news. No time — just keep doing what you're doing, *turn to page 108*

Get informed and read the news, *bookmark this page so you can return here and then turn to page 152*

AFTER YOU HAVE READ THE NEWS: YOU TURN FROM THE NEWS, YOUR COMMITMENT TO YOUR WORK REDOUBLED. WHAT DO YOU DECIDE TO DO NEXT?

Stay the course with the allies you have, *turn to page 108*
Organize a large gathering with new partners, *turn to page 127*

It was a Trump post on social media that triggered the Justice Department. Trump merely posted: "BENT-BACK MOVEMENT SHOULD BE IN JAIL FOR INCITEMENT." The next day, Justice Department officials released an error-ridden document with purported evidence of a "massive conspiracy." Two high-profile leaders are arrested with bail set at $2 million. Lawyers say the case is very flimsy — but because of its high political profile, it is hard to gauge how long it will go.

Lawyers say the government is only targeting a small set of movement leaders, not you personally. To avoid fear gripping the movement, you take a page from Black civil rights leaders who were targeted by the government of Montgomery, Alabama during the bus boycott in the 1950s. At first, leaders like Martin Luther King, Jr. went into hiding after vague threats of arrest based on antiquated anti-boycott laws. Then, movement organizer Bayard Rustin organized them to go down to the station and demand to be arrested since they were leaders — making a positive spectacle of the repression. So, like them, hundreds of strike leaders across the country descend on their attorneys general demanding their own arrests. ("We're leaders, too!"). You aren't arrested. But fear does not sink the movement.

Liberal pundits argue that Trump's just trying to distract from his sinking approval ratings or the shaky, whiplashed economy, suffering from all his changing policies. The movement feels more cautious. Trump's been given the go-ahead by the Supreme Court to replace 50,000 government workers under Schedule F. He's been installing judges at a fast rate — and gerrymandered maps now make long-term Republican control of power a distinct possibility.

The resistance wing is uncertain. You know you cannot do reactionary protests to everything he does — much less proposes. But many criticize the movement as too ineffective. The Paperclip Movement has hundreds of thousands of participants, at various levels. Some want to escalate by announcing the movement will make certain we have open and fair elections — on the bet Trump might prevent this. You wonder if you need a bigger perspective to see who is out there and where to find more energy.

DESPITE YOUR HARD WORK, IT'S HARD TO NOT SCAN THE EYE-CATCHING HEADLINES:

NEWS ALERTS: *POLICE ARREST LIZ CHENEY,*
TRUMP ENFORCES COMSTOCK ACT, ICE SHOOTS THREE IN STANDOFF...

Ignore the news. No time — just keep doing what you're doing, *turn to page 108*

Get informed and read the news, *bookmark this page so you can return here and then turn to page 152*

AFTER YOU HAVE READ THE NEWS: YOU TURN FROM THE NEWS, YOUR COMMITMENT TO YOUR WORK REDOUBLED. WHAT DO YOU DECIDE TO DO NEXT?

Stay the course with the allies you have, *turn to page 108*
Organize a large gathering with new partners, *turn to page 127*

The IRS tries to quietly freeze all the assets of the tax resistance committee. A high-ranking Paperclip Movement whistleblower tells you a story of insider intrigue over Trump's worry about your growing movement. Apparently, some Trump administrators argued against the IRS action, worried it would only continue to sink Trump's approval ratings. The argument that won was that this is a good way to shift attention away from the shaky economy — suffering whiplash from Trump's changing policies. "Trump's administration is in chaos. They want to stay in power forever," they say, "but they fear your movement."

For the next week the news is all consuming. The Paperclip Movement had wisely dispersed money among multiple organizational entities — so most is safe. But the website, database, and organizational infrastructure are temporarily immobilized. You spend late nights in emergency meetings to keep the infrastructure afloat. The Paperclip Movement holds.

The movement worries deeply it isn't building enough pressure. Trump's been given the go-ahead by the Supreme Court to replace 50,000 government workers under Schedule F. He's been installing judges at a fast rate — and gerrymandered maps now make long-term control of Republican power a distinct possibility. Sure, Trump's 16-week abortion ban is killed quickly in Congress by the movement's rapid direct action. And the courts handed Trump another setback when he ruled, for the second time, against his Mexican border bill. But Trump doubles down on everything. He vows to return the military to the border. Trump opens up the Arctic National Wildlife Refuge to drilling. He vows to "introduce an abortion bill that everyone will love."

The resistance wing is uncertain. You know you cannot do reactionary protests to everything he does — much less proposes. But many criticize the movement as too ineffective. The Paperclip Movement has hundreds of thousands of participants, at various levels. Some want to escalate by announcing the movement will make certain we have open and fair elections — on the bet Trump might prevent this. You wonder if you need a bigger perspective to see who is out there and where to find more energy.

DESPITE YOUR HARD WORK, IT'S HARD TO NOT SCAN THE EYE-CATCHING HEADLINES:
NEWS ALERTS: *POLICE ARREST LIZ CHENEY,*
TRUMP ENFORCES COMSTOCK ACT, ICE SHOOTS THREE IN STANDOFF...

Ignore the news. No time — just keep doing what you're doing, *turn to page 108*

Get informed and read the news, *bookmark this page so you can return here and then turn to page 152*

AFTER YOU HAVE READ THE NEWS: YOU TURN FROM THE NEWS, YOUR COMMITMENT TO YOUR WORK REDOUBLED. WHAT DO YOU DECIDE TO DO NEXT?

Stay the course with the allies you have, *turn to page 108*
Organize a large gathering with new partners, *turn to page 127*

Donald Trump ignores the protest movement. The Supreme Court allows him to proceed with firing 50,000 government workers under Schedule F. He fills the government with loyalists. Bureaucratic fights take place everywhere. Trump loyalists make life excruciating for institutionalists who remain, forcing resignations and further purgings. With control of multiple levers of government, Trump installs judges across the country who gerrymander election maps in multiple states to give Republicans long-term power.

It's not all loss. Trump floats a bill outlawing abortion after 16 weeks. The protest movement galvanizes direct actions all over the country. "Hands off my body." Congress halts the bill. Analysts point to Trump's decreasing approval ratings in the polls. And the courts hand Trump another setback when they rule, for the second time, against his bill to close the border with Mexico. As a result, the military again withdraws from policing the border.

But Trump doubles down on everything. He vows to return the military to the border. Emboldened right-wing militias echo ICE's mass deportation plans with frightful scenes of armed men strolling through immigrant neighborhoods. Trump opens up the Arctic National Wildlife Refuge to drilling. He vows to "introduce an abortion bill that everyone will love."

The resistance wing is uncertain. With Trump making so many moves, reactionary actions suck up much of the oxygen. As a result, the 15-minute strike only reaches the same number of people. Many criticize the movement as ineffective and in need of more allies. Others are urging it to keep on its path. You wonder if you need a bigger perspective to see who is out there and where to find more energy.

DESPITE YOUR HARD WORK, IT'S HARD TO NOT SCAN THE EYE-CATCHING HEADLINES:
NEWS ALERTS: *POLICE ARREST LIZ CHENEY, TRUMP ENFORCES COMSTOCK ACT, ICE SHOOTS THREE IN STANDOFF…*

Ignore the news. No time — just keep doing what you're doing, *turn to page 106*

Get informed and read the news, *bookmark this page so you can return here and then turn to page 152*

AFTER YOU HAVE READ THE NEWS: YOU TURN FROM THE NEWS, YOUR COMMITMENT TO YOUR WORK REDOUBLED. WHAT DO YOU DECIDE TO DO NEXT?

Stay the course with the allies you have, *turn to page 106*
Organize a large gathering with new partners, *turn to page 124*

Frustrated by reports of his falling approval ratings, Trump tests several lines of attack. "I will STRIKE back against the STRIKERS, trust me." When news of a shaky economy emerges, he blames your actions, "We could be a GREAT COUNTRY if people WORKED, NOT STRIKED." Amidst threats and taunts, he jeers that the strike was ineffective and writes, "I call it the LAZIEST STRIKE IN HISTORY." You wonder if his mind is slowing down.

The Supreme Court allows him to proceed with replacing 50,000 government workers under Schedule F with loyalists. His installs make life excruciating for government workers — but also for each other. Resignations and purgings are commonplace. With control of multiple levers of government, Trump installs judges across the country who gerrymander election maps in multiple states to give Republicans long-term power.

It's not all loss. Trump floats a bill outlawing abortion after 16 weeks. "Hands off my body." Congress halts the bill. Analysts point to Trump's decreasing approval ratings in the polls. And the courts hand Trump another setback when they rule, for the second time, against his bill to close the border with Mexico. As a result, the military again withdraws from policing the border.

But Trump doubles down on everything. He vows to return the military to the border. Emboldened right-wing militias echo ICE's mass deportation plans with frightful scenes of armed men strolling through immigrant neighborhoods. Trump opens up the Arctic National Wildlife Refuge to drilling. He vows to "introduce an abortion bill that everyone will love."

DESPITE YOUR HARD WORK, IT'S HARD TO NOT SCAN THE EYE-CATCHING HEADLINES:
NEWS ALERTS: *POLICE ARREST LIZ CHENEY,*
TRUMP ENFORCES COMSTOCK ACT, ICE SHOOTS THREE IN STANDOFF...

Ignore the news. No time — just keep doing what you're doing, *turn to page 106*

Get informed and read the news, *bookmark this page so you can return here and then turn to page 152*

AFTER YOU HAVE READ THE NEWS: YOU TURN FROM THE NEWS, YOUR COMMITMENT TO YOUR WORK REDOUBLED. WHAT DO YOU DECIDE TO DO NEXT?

Stay the course with the allies you have, *turn to page 106*
Organize a large gathering with new partners, *turn to page 124*

A Trump post on social media triggers the Justice Department to move against movement leaders. Trump merely posts: "TRAITOROUS STRIKERS SHOULD BE IN JAIL FOR INCITEMENT." The next day, Justice Department officials release an error-ridden document with purported evidence of a "massive conspiracy." Two high-profile strike leaders are arrested with bail set at $2 million. Lawyers say the case is very flimsy, but because of its high political profile, it is hard to gauge how long it will go.

Lawyers say the government is only targeting a small set of movement leaders, not you personally. To avoid fear gripping the movement, you take a page from Black civil rights leaders who were targeted by the government of Montgomery, Alabama during the bus boycott in the 1950s. At first, leaders like Martin Luther King, Jr. went into hiding after vague threats of arrest based on antiquated anti-boycott laws. Then, movement organizer Bayard Rustin organized them to go down to the station and demand to be arrested since they were leaders — making a positive spectacle of the repression. So, like them, hundreds of strike leaders across the country descend on their attorneys general demanding their own arrests. ("We're leaders, too!"). You aren't arrested. But fear does not sink the movement.

Liberal pundits argue that Trump's just trying to distract from his sinking approval ratings or the shaky, whiplashed economy, suffering from all his changing policies. The movement feels more cautious. Trump's been given the go-ahead by the Supreme Court to replace 50,000 government workers under Schedule F. He's been installing judges at a fast rate — and gerrymandered maps now make long-term Republican control of power a distinct possibility.

The resistance wing is uncertain. With Trump making so many moves, reactionary actions suck up much of the oxygen. As a result, the 15-minute strike only reaches the same number of people. Many criticize the movement as ineffective and in need of more allies. Others are urging it to keep on its path. You wonder if you need a bigger perspective to see who is out there and where to find more energy.

DESPITE YOUR HARD WORK, IT'S HARD TO NOT SCAN THE EYE-CATCHING HEADLINES:

NEWS ALERTS: *POLICE ARREST LIZ CHENEY, TRUMP ENFORCES COMSTOCK ACT, ICE SHOOTS THREE IN STANDOFF...*

Ignore the news. No time — just keep doing what you're doing, *turn to page 106*

Get informed and read the news, *bookmark this page so you can return here and then turn to page 152*

AFTER YOU HAVE READ THE NEWS: YOU TURN FROM THE NEWS, YOUR COMMITMENT TO YOUR WORK REDOUBLED. WHAT DO YOU DECIDE TO DO NEXT?

Stay the course with the allies you have, *turn to page 106*
Organize a large gathering with new partners, *turn to page 124*

On Trump's orders, the IRS tries to quietly freeze the assets of the Strike Committee. You alert a New York Times reporter, who broadcasts the news — telling a story of insider intrigue over Trump's worry about your growing movement. Apparently, some Trump administrators argued against the IRS action, worried it would only continue to sink Trump's approval ratings. The argument that won was that this is a good way to shift attention away from the shaky economy — suffering whiplash from Trump's changing policies.

His gambit failed. For the next week you stay in the news. The strike fund had wisely dispersed money among multiple organizational entities — so most is safe. But the website, database, and organizational infrastructure are temporarily immobilized. You spend late nights in emergency meetings to keep the infrastructure afloat. The Strike Committee holds, but you worry about capacity.

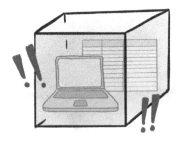

The movement worries deeply that it isn't building enough pressure. Trump's been given the go-ahead by the Supreme Court to replace 50,000 government workers under Schedule F. He's been installing judges at a fast rate — and gerrymandered maps now make long-term Republican control of power a distinct possibility. Sure, Trump's 16-week abortion ban is killed quickly in Congress thanks to the movement's rapid direct action. And the courts hand Trump another setback when they rule, for the second time, against his bill to close the border with Mexico. But Trump doubles down on everything. He vows to return the military to the border. He opens up the Arctic National Wildlife Refuge to drilling for oil. He vows to "introduce an abortion bill that everyone will love."

The resistance wing is uncertain. With Trump making so many moves, reactionary actions suck up much of the oxygen. As a result, the 15-minute strike only reaches the same number of people. Many criticize the movement as ineffective and in need of more allies. Others are urging it to keep on its path. You wonder if you need a bigger perspective to see who is out there and where to find more energy.

DESPITE YOUR HARD WORK, IT'S HARD TO NOT SCAN THE EYE-CATCHING HEADLINES:

NEWS ALERTS: *POLICE ARREST LIZ CHENEY,*
TRUMP ENFORCES COMSTOCK ACT, ICE SHOOTS THREE IN STANDOFF…

Ignore the news. No time — just keep doing what you're doing, *turn to page 106*

Get informed and read the news, *bookmark this page so you can return here and then turn to page 152*

AFTER YOU HAVE READ THE NEWS: YOU TURN FROM THE NEWS, YOUR COMMITMENT TO YOUR WORK REDOUBLED. WHAT DO YOU DECIDE TO DO NEXT?

Stay the course with the allies you have, *turn to page 106*
Organize a large gathering with new partners, *turn to page 124*

Donald Trump ignores the protest movement. The Supreme Court allows him to proceed with firing 50,000 government workers under Schedule F. He fills the government with loyalists. Bureaucratic fights take place everywhere. Trump loyalists make life excruciating for institutionalists who remain, forcing resignations and further purgings. With control of multiple levers of government, Trump installs judges across the country who gerrymander election maps in multiple states to give Republicans long-term power.

It's not all loss. Trump floats a bill outlawing abortion after 16 weeks. The protest movement galvanizes direct actions all over the country. "Hands off my body." Congress halts the bill. Analysts point to Trump's decreasing approval ratings in the polls. And the courts hand Trump another setback when they rule, for the second time, against his bill to close the border with Mexico. As a result, the military again withdraws from policing the border.

But Trump doubles down on everything. He vows to return the military to the border. Emboldened right-wing militias echo ICE's mass deportation plans with frightful scenes of armed men strolling through immigrant neighborhoods. Trump opens up the Arctic National Wildlife Refuge to drilling. He vows to "introduce an abortion bill that everyone will love."

The resistance wing is uncertain. With Trump making so many moves, reactionary actions suck up much of the oxygen. Many criticize the movement as ineffective and in need of more allies. Others are urging it to keep on its path. You wonder if you need a bigger perspective to see who is out there and where to find more energy.

DESPITE YOUR HARD WORK, IT'S HARD TO NOT SCAN THE EYE-CATCHING HEADLINES:
NEWS ALERTS: *POLICE ARREST LIZ CHENEY,*
TRUMP ENFORCES COMSTOCK ACT, ICE SHOOTS THREE IN STANDOFF...

Ignore the news. No time — just keep doing what you're doing, *turn to page 107*

Get informed and read the news, *bookmark this page so you can return here and then turn to page 152*

AFTER YOU HAVE READ THE NEWS: YOU TURN FROM THE NEWS, YOUR COMMITMENT TO YOUR WORK REDOUBLED. WHAT DO YOU DECIDE TO DO NEXT?

Stay the course with the allies you have, *turn to page 107*
Organize a large gathering with new partners, *turn to page 128*

Frustrated by reports of his falling approval rating, Trump tests several lines of attack. "We don't need their TAXES." When news of the shaky economy emerges, he turns back to your actions, "We could be a GREAT COUNTRY if not for TAX-DODGING LAW-BREAKERS." You wonder if his mind is slowing down.

The Supreme Court allows him to proceed with firing 50,000 government workers under Schedule F. He fills the government with loyalists. Bureaucratic fights take place everywhere. It's not all loss. Trump floats a bill outlawing abortion after 16 weeks. The protest movement galvanizes direct actions all over the country. "Hands off my body." Congress halts the bill. Analysts point to Trump's decreasing approval ratings in the polls. And the courts hand Trump another setback when they rule, for the second time, against his bill to close the border with Mexico. As a result, the military again withdraws from policing the border.

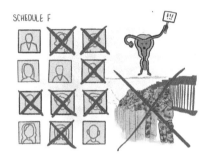

But Trump doubles down on everything. He vows to return the military to the border. Emboldened right-wing militias echo ICE's mass deportation plans with frightful scenes of armed men strolling through immigrant neighborhoods. Trump opens up the Arctic National Wildlife Refuge to drilling. He vows to "introduce an abortion bill that everyone will love."

The resistance wing is uncertain. You know you cannot do reactionary protests to everything he does — much less proposes. Over 200,000 people have withheld their taxes, many in an escrow "until the next President." Now that April 15th is past, movement energy is dragging. You wonder if you need a bigger perspective to see who is out there and where to find more energy.

DESPITE YOUR HARD WORK, IT'S HARD TO NOT SCAN THE EYE-CATCHING HEADLINES:
NEWS ALERTS: *POLICE ARREST LIZ CHENEY,*
TRUMP ENFORCES COMSTOCK ACT, ICE SHOOTS THREE IN STANDOFF…

Ignore the news. No time — just keep doing what you're doing, *turn to page 107*

Get informed and read the news, *bookmark this page so you can return here and then turn to page 152*

AFTER YOU HAVE READ THE NEWS: YOU TURN FROM THE NEWS, YOUR COMMITMENT TO YOUR WORK REDOUBLED. WHAT DO YOU DECIDE TO DO NEXT?

Stay the course with the allies you have, *turn to page 107*
Organize a large gathering with new partners, *turn to page 128*

A Trump post on social media triggers the Justice Department to move against movement leaders. Trump merely posts: "TAX DODGERS SHOULD BE CHARGED AS TRAITORS." The next day, Justice Department officials release an error-ridden document with purported evidence of a "massive conspiracy." Two high-profile strike leaders are arrested with bail set at $2 million. Lawyers say the case is very flimsy, but because of its high political profile, it is hard to gauge how long it will go.

Lawyers say the government is only targeting a small set of movement leaders, not you personally. To avoid fear gripping the movement, you take a page from Black civil rights leaders who were targeted by the government of Montgomery, Alabama during the bus boycott in the 1950s. At first, leaders like Martin Luther King, Jr. went into hiding after vague threats of arrest based on antiquated anti-boycott laws. Then, movement organizer Bayard Rustin organized them to go down to the station and demand to be arrested since they were leaders — making a positive spectacle of the repression. So, like them, hundreds of strike leaders across the country descend on their attorneys general demanding their own arrests. ("We're leaders, too!"). You aren't arrested. But fear does not sink the movement.

Liberal pundits argue that Trump's just trying to distract from his sinking approval ratings or the shaky, whiplashed economy, suffering from all his changing policies. The movement feels more cautious. Trump's been given the go-ahead by the Supreme Court to replace 50,000 government workers under Schedule F. He's been installing judges at a fast rate — and gerrymandered maps now make long-term Republican control of power a distinct possibility.

The resistance wing is uncertain. You know you cannot do reactionary protests to everything he does — much less proposes. Over 200,000 people have withheld their taxes, many in an escrow "until the next President." Now that April 15th is past, movement energy is dragging. You wonder if you need a bigger perspective to see who is out there and where to find more energy.

DESPITE YOUR HARD WORK, IT'S HARD TO NOT SCAN THE EYE-CATCHING HEADLINES:

NEWS ALERTS: *POLICE ARREST LIZ CHENEY, TRUMP ENFORCES COMSTOCK ACT, ICE SHOOTS THREE IN STANDOFF...*

Ignore the news. No time — just keep doing what you're doing, *turn to page 107*

Get informed and read the news, *bookmark this page so you can return here and then turn to page 152*

AFTER YOU HAVE READ THE NEWS: YOU TURN FROM THE NEWS, YOUR COMMITMENT TO YOUR WORK REDOUBLED. WHAT DO YOU DECIDE TO DO NEXT?

Stay the course with the allies you have, *turn to page 107*
Organize a large gathering with new partners, *turn to page 128*

On Trump's orders, the IRS tries to quietly freeze all the assets of the tax resistance committee, emptying the offices of computers, files, and even the coffee pots. They want it to be a terrifying story. Your colleague alerts a New York Times reporter, who broadcasts the news — telling a story of insider intrigue over Trump's worry about your growing movement. Apparently, some Trump administrators argued against the IRS action, worried it would only continue to sink Trump's approval ratings. The argument that won was that this is a good way to shift attention away from the shaky economy — suffering whiplash from Trump's changing policies.

That night your team meets. Some are terrified that the publicility makes you look weak and will frighten supporters. You come up with an alternative. The next day you make a very public "reentry" into your offices with a moving van full of boxes. Media trail you. As expected, police stop the van and take the boxes. This turns to humiliation as they lift the boxes…and find them all empty. "This administration is fearful of everything." You then spend many late nights in emergency meetings to keep the infrastructure afloat. The Tax Resistance Movement holds.

The movement worries deeply it isn't building enough pressure. Trump's been given the go-ahead by the Supreme Court to replace 50,000 government workers under Schedule F. He's been installing judges at a fast rate — and gerrymandered maps now make long-term control of Republican power a distinct possibility. Sure, Trump's 16-week abortion ban is killed quickly in Congress by the movement's rapid direct action. And the courts hand Trump another setback when it rules, for the second time, against his Mexican border bill. But Trump doubles down on everything. He vows to return the military to the border. Trump opens up the Arctic National Wildlife Refuge to drilling. He vows to "introduce an abortion bill that everyone will love."

The resistance wing is uncertain. You know you cannot do reactionary protests to everything he does — much less proposes. But many criticize the movement as too ineffective. Over 150,000 people have withheld their taxes, many in an escrow "until the next President." With your action, only 12,000 people unsign the petition. Now that April 15th is past, movement energy is dragging. You wonder if you need a bigger perspective to see who is out there and where to find more energy.

DESPITE YOUR HARD WORK, IT'S HARD TO NOT SCAN THE EYE-CATCHING HEADLINES:
NEWS ALERTS: *POLICE ARREST LIZ CHENEY, TRUMP ENFORCES COMSTOCK ACT, ICE SHOOTS THREE IN STANDOFF...*

Ignore the news. No time — just keep doing what you're doing, *turn to page 107*

Get informed and read the news, *bookmark this page so you can return here and then turn to page 152*

AFTER YOU HAVE READ THE NEWS: YOU TURN FROM THE NEWS, YOUR COMMITMENT TO YOUR WORK REDOUBLED. WHAT DO YOU DECIDE TO DO NEXT?

Stay the course with the allies you have, *turn to page 107*
Organize a large gathering with new partners, *turn to page 128*

You are asked to join a meeting for some key members of the Strike Committee. They have organized a 1-minute national strike — with almost a million people participating. They want to reach out to other movement sectors, like getting poll workers to agree to participate in a strike if the elections are not actually free and fair. You're honestly not sure why you're present — they seem to have a good strategy and good sensibility. But you can sense the frenetic pace that you've seen everywhere.

After a lunch break, one member of the Strike Committee urges everyone, "We just have to double down and do a national strike now — Trump isn't going to let us have a real election." He cites unnamed sources inside the White House discussing Trump's plans to stay in office. One source said Trump was discussing running for a third term — despite the 22nd Amendment, which explicitly forbids this. (Trump allegedly yelled, "Who's gonna stop me?") Another source suggested that Eric Trump might run as a surrogate, or perhaps Trump would just declare a state of emergency to halt elections for as long as possible. The Strike Committee member is urgent, "This is it. We have to throw everything at this or we lose whatever version of democracy we have."

To everyone's surprise, you stand up. You hold your hands out. "You're absolutely right. You have to move. And you have to move fast. But you have to be smart — you can't go into this breathless. I want everyone to take a breath before you do." You take a breath and notice that nobody else really joins you. "I'm serious. You have been at a breakneck speed already. Take a breath." A few do. "Before you head into this course, you need to have the whole movement ground itself."

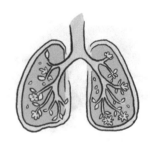

Taking cues from your intervention, the group decides to clear all activity from its calendar for one weekend. They don't universally take time off, but even that bit of reduced activity allows new behaviors. Without scheduled actions, some organizers have time to reach out to new allies, and others reconnect with their passions. All report the time opened them up to new options — and made them feel even more convinced that a nationwide strike is ready to go forward.

THEY ASK YOU TO JOIN. DO YOU ATTEND?

Do not attend the Strike Committee meeting, *turn to page 123*
Join with the Strike resistance movement, *turn to page 124*

By the first hour of your first local convention, you are glad you were heavily trained in participatory budgeting and facilitation. People aren't used to democratic spaces, so some people came just to argue or expecting to sound off. "If you don't want a democracy, keep shouting. But a democracy means we talk and listen," you calmly affirm. You explain there will be three day-long sessions: one to learn from each other, one to make proposals and discuss them, and a third to vote on proposals. The first day goes well.

Even more people arrive for the second session. This day is a tricky, day-long session where people make proposals for how the Constitution needs to be changed along with making affirmations. New people arrive without the context from the first meeting — but others urge them to listen. The process smooths out and a truly democratic thing is happening — people are learning about their laws, debating policy, and making serious proposals.

By the last session, the community is hooked. You listen to a myriad of proposals and then voting happens. The town comes out in droves, almost rivaling some elections in terms of turnout. Like at a science fair, people walk around and hear debates over different proposals. Others join online. On a large electronic board, people can see the results of voting coming in from other towns, too.

Most of the results don't surprise you. Certain measures pass by large margins: eliminating money from politics, limiting terms for judges and senators, ending secret holds and the filibuster, breaking apart the two-party system, and (surprising to some) creating a pathway to citizenship for undocumented immigrants. Other measures remain hotly debated: anything around gun laws, crime reduction strategies, and other aspects of immigration. Those are saved for future conventions to allow this movement to focus on the most widely shared issues. You feel very satisfied — tired, but pleased.

YOU ARE WALKING HOME WHEN A FRIEND TEXTS URGENTLY.

Read the text message, *turn to page 119*

After a militia burns several local Black businesses, you help relocate a local businessman who believes he's a primary target. Each case is hard and painful. Nobody wants to be uprooted from a place. But survival can be an act of courage. Their bravery inspires you to step into more national networking across the Underground Railroad. The primary need is more open conductors — people who "everyone knows" can help get people into the Underground Railroad. These people need to be willing to face harassment and be precise about digital security.

You host open online trainings to recruit conductors — but that doesn't bring in the right people. You eventually decide to network through existing religious institutions. You find strong allies inside Black churches, Quaker Meetings, Jewish synagogues, and Muslim mosques — all groups who have a history of doing work like this. You expand training on digital security and personal safety.

Even though your work can feel heavy, it feels almost optimistic, starkly different from the toxic political environment. Over the next year, you see small political changes around you. But it feels like barely a dent amidst the national scene. Despite lower poll numbers, Trump continues filling the government with his loyalists. The courts eventually approve his Schedule F reclassification — 50,000 government workers are now being systematically replaced by Trump loyalists. Bureaucratic fights rage across many institutions. Trump installs judges across the country who gerrymander election maps in multiple states to give Republicans long-term power. But your heart tears as you see the language of fear and violence growing: immigrant communities terrified by right-wing militia patrols, increased violence against peaceful protestors, attacks on emissions standards, and exaggerated calls for political arrests.

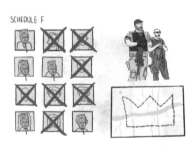

YOU ARE WALKING HOME WHEN A FRIEND TEXTS URGENTLY.

Read the text message, *turn to page 115*

You run around the country growing local conventions. A lot of your time is spent traveling and meeting in community centers. You can't remember the number of times you explain: "There are three legs to democracy: representation, education, and participation. Being represented by officials through a free and fair election is critical — but that's not all Democracy is — we have to grow the other legs to have a healthy, stable Democracy." The Constitutional Convention is a rare opportunity for education and participation.

You explain the process, drawn from participatory budgeting and other participatory methodology: three day-long sessions: one day to learn about the Constitution and to analyze its strengths and weaknesses, one day to debate and propose changes or affirmations, and a final day to review the proposals and vote. On that last day, like a science fair, people walk around and hear people arguing for different proposals. On a large electronic board, people can see the results coming in from towns all over. You personally help run 43 sessions.

Most of the results don't surprise you. Certain measures pass by large margins: eliminating money from politics, limiting terms for judges and senators, ending secret holds and the filibuster, breaking apart the two-party system, and (surprising to some) creating a pathway to citizenship for undocumented immigrants. Other measures remain hotly debated: anything around gun laws, crime reduction strategies, and other aspects of immigration. Those are saved for future conventions to allow this movement to focus on the most widely shared issues. You feel very satisfied — tired, but pleased.

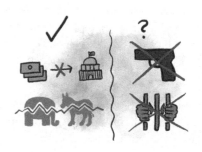

YOU ARE WALKING HOME WHEN A FRIEND TEXTS URGENTLY.

Read the text message, *turn to page 119*

You join a group going back into the streets to confront MAGA supporters directly. Few join the protest, scared by the violence. You have one goal: to make sure MAGA can't take the streets unchallenged. You're fine with the action being chaotic. The National Guard does not bother you. The police order you to disperse, citing the state of emergency and curfews. You escape them and find some MAGA breakaway groups. You get into yelling matches, which escalate into scuffles.

You arrive home exhausted. News reports intersperse video of your action with other scenes of violence. Your feeling of standing up for your community looks blurry in the news. Your actions haven't differentiated your tactics from your message. The media frames your action as "ANTIFA violence added to the heat." You remain proud that you stood up for your rights — and that you didn't succumb to fear in the midst of it all.

But you see this doesn't translate very well into political achievements. In the minds of the general public, the street violence only strengthened the justification for the military to take control. You wish you had better remembered you're not fighting for control of the streets — you're fighting for legitimacy. And with the chaotic violence, nobody got that point.

Thousands are arrested, including many National Guard members and police who sided with Trump. The situation remains extremely tense and reports of targeted violence remain. On January 20th, President Harris is inaugurated. The coup never wins legitimacy and has been averted. Donald Trump's court cases catch up with him and he is imprisoned. But the work of creating a much stronger, more robust democracy remains.

You survived the transfer of power, but you could have been more efficient. Researcher Stephen Zunes has identified four things we need to stop a coup: widespread opposition, nonviolent discipline (to avoid giving the wanna-be autocrat excuses for more violence), alliance building, and refusal to recognize the coup plotters as legitimate. In a coup situation, you don't confront the extreme — you speak to the middle.

Try again — or turn to Closing, page 156

It's hard work, but people across the nation want to do something to stand up for democracy. National organizers pull together a one-minute national strike. At 12 noon EST, all work is to be temporarily stopped for one minute. Doctors go on breaks. Transit halts across the country. Truck drivers pull off to the side of the road. Where you are, people don't join as much as you'd hoped. But when you watch videos of people frozen while walking down the street, it does your heart good. You realize you are not alone.

The opposition media smears your efforts. But too many people participated themselves or at least knew people who were participants in the one-minute action — the media attacks don't convince anyone but die-hard MAGA. The strike strengthens mainstream institutions, like the military, which now actively purges coup supporters. Emboldened, the national Strike Committee announces plans for a longer, 15-minute strike in the next week — with plans to ramp up toward a full general strike if necessary.

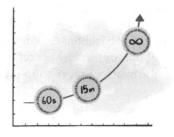

The threats of a full strike aren't needed. Boosted by the widespread strikes and ensuing protests in the streets, the military apparatus and Harris and Biden regain full control of the National Guard. Thousands are arrested, including many National Guard members and police. The situation remains extremely tense, with continued reports of targeted violence. On January 20th, President Harris is inaugurated. The coup never won legitimacy and has been averted. Donald Trump's court cases catch up with him and he is imprisoned. But the work of creating a much stronger, robust democracy remains.

THE END

You survived the transfer of power. But creating a deep democracy is a much bigger task ahead. Researcher Stephen Zunes has identified four things we need to stop a coup: widespread opposition, nonviolent discipline (to avoid giving the wanna-be autocrat excuses for more violence), alliance building, and refusal to recognize the coup plotters as legitimate.

Try again — or turn to Closing, page 156

You hear about the pro-democracy movement announcing massive demonstrations on January 16th, ahead of the inauguration. You call as many friends as you can to go together to Washington, D.C. — enough for a large bus. When you arrive, the streets are packed. People from across the political spectrum show up — from radical left-wingers with piercings and tattoos to buttoned-down D.C. bureaucrats. Almost 300,000 people throng to D.C. Even more join locally organized protests.

The opposition media smears the efforts. But the media attacks don't convince anyone but diehard MAGA. The mass rally strengthens mainstream institutions' backbones. Retired generals come out in fierce support for "the peaceful transfer of power" and the military purges coup supporters.

Boosted by the widespread strikes and ensuing protests in the streets, the National Guard is put back into control by the military. Thousands are arrested, including many National Guard members and police. The situation remains extremely tense, with reports of sporadic violence. However, on January 20th, President Harris is inaugurated. Donald Trump's court cases catch up with him and he is imprisoned. A successful coup has been averted. But the work of creating a much stronger, robust democracy remains.

THE END

You survived the transfer of power. But creating a deep democracy is a much bigger task ahead. Researcher Stephen Zunes has identified four things we need to stop a coup: widespread opposition, nonviolent discipline (to avoid giving the wanna-be autocrat excuses for more violence), alliance building, and refusal to recognize the coup plotters as legitimate.

Try again — or turn to Closing, page 156

You decide to just let this play out. The Army ends up fighting prolonged street battles with MAGA supporters and the National Guard. The violence gravely deteriorates the country's international standing.

You realize the lack of an active pro-democracy movement has created long-term problems. The military generals are permanently seen as political forces, capable of deciding future elections. Anyone seeking the office of president now has to have secret meetings with military elites to seek their approval. This undermines the government. You wish people had gone into the street — in any way — so it didn't seem like the military was acting unilaterally.

Eventually, Biden, Harris, and the military do regain control. Thousands are arrested, including many National Guard members and police. The situation remains extremely tense, with reports of targeted violence. On January 20th, President Harris is inaugurated. Donald Trump's court cases catch up with him and he is imprisoned. A successful coup has been averted, but a true democracy remains further away.

THE END

You survived the transfer of power, but by leaning on the military instead of on people power. Researcher Stephen Zunes has identified four things we need to stop a coup: widespread opposition, nonviolent discipline (to avoid giving the wanna-be autocrat excuses for more violence), alliance building, and refusal to recognize the coup plotters as legitimate. In a coup situation, we need to be in the streets — and fast.

Try again — or turn to Closing, page 156

Your group decides it's time to escalate now. You put out a call for full disobedience on all social media channels and to everyone you talk with. But people are reluctant to join, and your worry grows that the call was premature.

During the weeks leading up to the strike, you try to warn people that not enough organizing has happened. Hundreds of college campuses are prepared, and a few local unions and minor groups sign up. But only two national unions endorse the strike — with more publicly rebuffing the efforts. Most of the people joining have already been in the disobedience camp.

On strike day — February 21st — the weakness of your movement is exposed. Far less than 0.3% of the population join. Trump moves fast to dismantle the movement. With very little political backing and media calling it weak, you can tell the movement is overexposed. Some movement leaders manage to get underground, but many others are rounded up and arrested on trumped up charges. You are spared — but you watch as the movement disintegrates.

You feel this outcome was preventable. The tactic was right, but the timing was off. Pulling off a strike requires a lot of preparation and buy-in from a wide segment of society. But this time, it's too late. Trump maintains his grip on power. His family remains in power for decades.

The autocrat won this time. But you can try again. Unfortunately, it is true that movements can get stuck in one tactic or a single approach. To speak to new people, however, they often have to switch it up — and knowing when to do that isn't always obvious.

Try again — or turn to Closing, page 156

Your group carries on its work. It adds more people day by day. But it's hard to maintain a tax resistance campaign that generates new press, especially after April 15th. You still have a big list — hundreds of thousands who have resisted paying taxes — but you have few allies and no clear way to grow.

You try to persuade people to get more strategic and look for opportunities to connect with other groups. But you feel like a window of opportunity was missed. In the fight against an authoritarian regime, at some point the movement needs to "call the question" — to unite all the forces in a single push. The movement never finds the right moment.

Trump moves quickly and quietly to dismantle the movement, directing the IRS to investigate many of its top leaders. Some are quietly arrested as others are hit with gigantic tax charges. With very little political backing and media calling the movement weak, the movement isn't able to weather the attack this time.

You feel this was preventable. The tactic was right, but the timing was off. Tax resistance can work, but pulling it off requires adjusting tactics over time and getting buy-in from a wider segment of society. But this time, it's too late. Trump maintains his grip on power. His family remains in power for decades.

THE END

The autocrat won this time. But you can try again. Unfortunately, it is true that movements can get stuck in one tactic or a single approach. To speak to new people, however, they often have to switch it up — and knowing when to do that isn't always obvious.

Try again — or turn to Closing, page 156

The movement continues to experience a trickle of growth — a few people day by day. You have a big list of people agreeing to resist Trump — but it's largely confined to anti-Trumpers. There's no clear way to grow outside that circle.

You try to persuade people to get more strategic and look for opportunities to connect with other groups. But you feel like a window of opportunity was missed. In the fight against an authoritarian regime, at some point the movement needs to "call the question" — to unite all the forces in a single push. The movement never finds the right moment.

Sensing its exposed position, Trump moves quickly and quietly to dismantle the movement. Trump orders a counterintelligence operation that exposes many members of the Paperclip Movement. Some are quietly arrested as others are hit with gigantic tax bills. The movement isn't able to weather the attack this time.

You feel this was preventable. The tactic was right — but the problem of growth is too critical. You realize the movement needed to keep finding new allies. But this time, it's too late. Trump maintains his grip on power. His family remains in power for decades.

THE END

The autocrat won this time. But you can try again. Unfortunately, it is true that movements can get stuck in one tactic or a single approach. To speak to new people, however, they often have to switch it up — and knowing when to do that isn't always obvious.

Try again — or turn to Closing, page 156

You decide it's best to stay small and not talk openly about your work. Being quiet allows you to have some intimate conversations with people inside the military you might miss if you are more open. Plus, you see many friends burning out by constantly "doing more" to halt the ongoing Trump pronouncements. You resist that tendency. You do your small part and feel good about it.

Your organizing with veteran families gains quiet victories that the history books will never cover. One wife of a colonel confides in you that she worries her husband is sympathizing too much with those who urge fully enacting Trump's orders. But you give her some suggestions of things to do to help steady him. Later, she says it worked. Several families of noncommissioned officers decide to expose some Trump extremists in their ranks who plan to use the cover of a right-wing attack on local Black businesses for more extreme efforts.

Over the next year, you see small political changes around you. But it feels like barely a dent amidst the national scene. Despite lower poll numbers, Trump continues filling the government with his loyalists. The courts eventually approve his Schedule F reclassification — 50,000 government workers are now being systematically replaced by Trump loyalists. Bureaucratic fights rage across many institutions. Trump installs judges across the country who gerrymander election maps in multiple states to give Republicans long-term power. But your heart tears as you see the language of fear and violence growing: immigrant communities terrified by right-wing militia patrols, increased violence against peaceful protestors, attacks on emissions standards, and exaggerated calls for political arrests. But at least the military is not out among them.

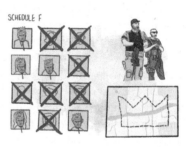

SCHEDULE F

YOU ARE WALKING HOME WHEN A FRIEND TEXTS URGENTLY.

Read the text message, *turn to page 118*

You decide to open your network to more people and make it public. You secure your personal information and take several digital security classes to avoid being doxxed. You're immediately rewarded with more veteran family volunteers joining your efforts right away and a robust social media profile.

Your organizing with veteran families gains quiet victories that the history books will never cover. One wife of a colonel confides in you that she worries her husband is sympathizing too much with those who urge fully enacting Trump's orders. But you give her some suggestions of things to do to help steady him. Later, she says it worked. You're able to bring her into a network of other families who actively find people who need to be shored up. In another case, families of noncommissioned officers decide to expose some Trump extremists in their ranks who plan to use the cover of a right-wing attack on local Black businesses for more extreme efforts. Though your work is public, the outreach itself is quiet — and very effective.

Over the next year, you see small political changes around you. But it feels like barely a dent amidst the national scene. Despite lower poll numbers, Trump continues filling the government with his loyalists. The courts eventually approve his Schedule F reclassification — 50,000 government workers are now being systematically replaced by Trump loyalists. Bureaucratic fights rage across many institutions. Trump installs judges across the country who gerrymander election maps in multiple states to give Republicans long-term power. But your heart tears as you see the language of fear and violence growing: immigrant communities terrified by right-wing militia patrols, increased violence against peaceful protestors, attacks on emissions standards, and exaggerated calls for political arrests. But at least the military is not out among them.

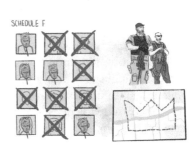

YOU ARE WALKING HOME WHEN A FRIEND TEXTS URGENTLY.

Read the text message, *turn to page 118*

You decide it's best to stay small and not talk openly about your work. Being quiet allows you to have some intimate conversations you might miss if you are more open. Plus, you see many friends burning out by constantly "doing more" to halt the ongoing Trump pronouncements. You resist that tendency. You do your small part and feel good about it.

Through your research, you are able to get some changes made here and there. Due to your research, your town rewrote its ordinances to plant more trees and (at least temporarily) halt expansion of some factories. The EPA, one of the most recognized and appreciated divisions of the government, is underfunded but able to continue to do their work. When a climate-change-fueled fire burns through your city, you are able to provide real-time tracking and data that's vital for people's health and safety.

Over the next year, you see small political changes around you. But it feels like barely a dent amidst the national scene. Despite lower poll numbers, Trump continues filling the government with his loyalists. The courts eventually approve his Schedule F reclassification — 50,000 government workers are now being systematically replaced by Trump loyalists. Bureaucratic fights rage across many institutions. Trump installs judges across the country who gerrymander election maps in multiple states to give Republicans long-term power. But your heart tears as you see the language of fear and violence growing: immigrant communities terrified by right-wing militia patrols, increased violence against peaceful protestors, attacks on emissions standards, and exaggerated calls for political arrests.

YOU ARE WALKING HOME WHEN A FRIEND TEXTS URGENTLY.

Read the text message, *turn to page 120*

You decide to open your network to more people and make it public. You secure your personal information and take several digital security classes, to avoid doxxing. You're immediately rewarded with more volunteers right away and a robust social media profile. When a climate change-fueled fire burns through your city, you are able to provide real-time tracking and data that's vital for people's health and safety.

You spend more time coordinating, training, and providing resources across the country for people looking to set up their own environmental testing. Distrust of government is high, and you find people of all stripes interested in participating. You find funding from a university with a small staff and lots of free student interns to help carry out this quiet mission. In small part thanks to your work, the EPA, one of the most recognized and appreciated divisions of the government, is able to continue to do their work effectively.

Over the next year you see small positive changes around you. But it feels like barely a dent amidst the national scene. Despite lower poll numbers, Trump continues filling all of the government with his loyalists. The courts eventually approve his Schedule F reclassification — 50,000 government workers are now being systematically replaced by Trump loyalists. Bureaucratic fights rage across many institutions. Trump installs judges across the country and gerrymanders multiple states for long-term control of Republican power. But your heart tears as you see the language of fear and violence growing: migrant communities terrified by right-wing militia patrols, increased violence against peaceful protestors, attacks on emissions standards, and exaggerated calls for political arrests.

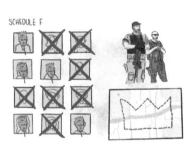

YOU ARE WALKING HOME WHEN A FRIEND TEXTS URGENTLY.

Read the text message, *turn to page 120*

You decide it's best to stay small. This allows you to prioritize your work locally. Plus, you see many friends burning out by constantly "doing more" to halt the ongoing Trump pronouncements. You resist that tendency. You do your part and feel good about it.

There's no clearinghouse for grant opportunities, and few officials have much time to research. So you develop an extensive spreadsheet of all the possible resources you can find. You hand the spreadsheet off to other election integrity folks and — within those circles — it goes viral. You see modest strengthening of the election infrastructure — better defended against cyberattacks, but also better prepared for all events. When a climate-change-fueled fire burns through the city, they are able to redeliver mail-in ballots quickly. Rather than just waiting until after the election to explain how the process is secure, you are able to demonstrate the safety, security, and responsiveness of the election infrastructure for all to see.

Over the next year, you see small political changes around you. But it feels like barely a dent amidst the national scene. Despite lower poll numbers, Trump continues filling the government with his loyalists. The courts eventually approve his Schedule F reclassification — 50,000 government workers are now being systematically replaced by Trump loyalists. Bureaucratic fights rage across many institutions. Trump installs judges across the country who gerrymander election maps in multiple states to give Republicans long-term power. But your heart tears as you see the language of fear and violence growing: immigrant communities terrified by right-wing militia patrols, increased violence against peaceful protestors, attacks on emissions standards, and exaggerated calls for political arrests.

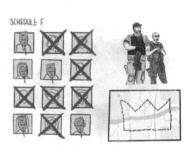

SCHEDULE F

YOU ARE WALKING HOME WHEN A FRIEND TEXTS URGENTLY.

Read the text message, *turn to page 121*

You decide to open your network to more people and make it public. You secure your personal information and take several digital security classes, to avoid doxxing. You're immediately rewarded with more volunteers right away and a robust social media profile.

You develop an extensive spreadsheet of possible resources and a website where people can quickly pre-qualify for grants based on data like their size or location. You are now the best national clearinghouse for grant opportunities. Your resources go viral in election integrity circles. You see elections getting stronger — both better defended against cyberattacks, but also better able to articulate how robust they are. When a climate-change-fueled fire burns through the city, they are able to redeliver mail-in ballots quickly. Rather than just waiting until after the election to explain how the process is secure, you demonstrate the safety, security, and responsiveness for all to see.

Over the next year, you see small political changes around you. But it feels like barely a dent amidst the national scene. Despite lower poll numbers, Trump continues filling the government with his loyalists. The courts eventually approve his Schedule F reclassification — 50,000 government workers are now being systematically replaced by Trump loyalists. Bureaucratic fights rage across many institutions. Trump installs judges across the country who gerrymander election maps in multiple states to give Republicans long-term power. But your heart tears as you see the language of fear and violence growing: immigrant communities terrified by right-wing militia patrols, increased violence against peaceful protestors, attacks on emissions standards, and exaggerated calls for political arrests.

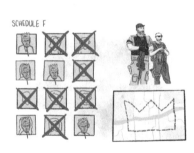

YOU ARE WALKING HOME WHEN A FRIEND TEXTS URGENTLY.

Read the text message, *turn to page 121*

Your friend texts you, "Did you see? Trump's gonna try to stay in power!" You click the link to see what she's talking about. You scan quickly. In Trump's style, he says the quiet part out loud at a midterm rally, "You don't want me going to jail. But the CROOKED COURTS are trying. If I have to, I'll stay President until the courts drop all my cases!"

It goes on to cite unnamed sources inside the White House. One source said Trump was discussing running for a third term — despite the 22nd Amendment, which forbids a President from holding a third term. "Who's gonna stop me?" Another source suggested that Eric Trump might run as a surrogate or perhaps Trump just orders a state of emergency to halt elections for as long as possible. Your heart clenches at any of these possibilities.

Before you get a chance to process, a longstanding volunteer calls you. Though they've been a steady volunteer, you know most of their work is with the resistance movement. "We've done those national one-minute work slowdowns." You nod. You're aware of them but have never participated. "It's about to explode — and we need people to join the next one-day national strike. Will you join us for a meeting at least?" You nod quietly. You see the potential, but you've been trying to keep people safe. And this movement is risking people being less safe. "We have a plan. Help us?"

YOU SEE WHAT THEY'RE DOING AND TRUST THEY'RE FOR REAL. BUT IT'S A BIG RISK. DO YOU JOIN THEM?

Do not join with other groups, *turn to page 122*
Join with the Strike resistance movement, *turn to page 124*

Your friend texts you, "Did you see? Trump's gonna try to stay in power!" You click the link to see what she's talking about. You scan quickly. In Trump's style, he says the quiet part out loud at a midterm rally, "You don't want me going to jail. But the CROOKED COURTS are trying. If I have to, I'll stay President until the courts drop all my cases!"

It goes on to cite unnamed sources inside the White House. One source said Trump was discussing running for a third term — despite the 22nd Amendment, which forbids a President from holding a third term. "Who's gonna stop me?" Another source suggested that Eric Trump might run as a surrogate or perhaps Trump just orders a state of emergency to halt elections for as long as possible. Your heart clenches at any of these possibilities.

Before you get a chance to process, a longstanding volunteer calls you. Though they've been a steady volunteer, you know most of their work is with the Paperclip Movement. "We've done those national 1-minute work slow-downs." You nod, aware of them but never have participated. "It's about to explode — and we need everyone to join the next one-day national strike. Will you join us for a meeting at least?" You nod quietly. You see the potential, but you've been trying to keep people safe. And this movement is risking people being less safe. "We have a plan. Help us?"

YOU SEE WHAT THEY'RE DOING AND TRUST THEY'RE FOR REAL. BUT IT'S A BIG RISK. DO YOU JOIN THEM?

Do not join with other groups, *turn to page 122*
Join with the Strike resistance movement, *turn to page 124*

Your friend texts you, "Did you see? Trump's announced he's ordering electric vehicle plants to shut down?!" You click the link to see what she's talking about and scan the article quickly. You vaguely remember that when talking about electric vehicles (EVs), Trump promised a "bloodbath" if his oppoennt was elected. Trump's base has soured on EVs, seeing them as part of the "woke agenda." Trump has now invoked the Defense Production Act to repurpose EV plants to produce gasoline-engine vehicles.

The article cites unnamed sources inside the White House. An unnamed economic advisor calls the move "backward," noting that over 100,000 jobs in the EV sector would be threatened by Trump's new policy, which attempts to undo plans that auto producers have already put in motion. Another source calls it "just a stunt," explaining that "you can't repurpose an EV plant by an order." Autoworkers are furious.

Before you get a chance to process, a longstanding volunteer calls you. Though they've been a steady volunteer, you know most of their work is with the resistance movement. "The resistance has gotten tens of thousands of people to refuse to pay taxes, including several major businesses. We think there's an opportunity for further action to keep the EV industry operating despite the Defense Production Act, but it may get violent and we need help making sure nothing gets out of hand." You nod quietly. You see the potential, but this movement has a history of being … illegal… and a very different kind of work. "We have a plan. Help us?"

YOU'RE CURIOUS WHAT THEY'RE DOING AND TRUST THEY'RE FOR REAL. BUT IT'S A BIG RISK. DO YOU JOIN THEM?

Do not join with other groups, *turn to page 122*
Join with the Resistance to support EV workers, *turn to page 125*

Your friend texts you, "Did you see? Trump's announced he's ordering electric vehicle plants to shut down?!" You click the link to see what she's talking about and scan the article quickly. You vaguely remember that when talking about electric vehicles (EVs), Trump promised a "bloodbath" if his opponent was elected. Trump's base has soured on EVs, seeing them as part of the "woke agenda." Trump has now invoked the Defense Production Act to repurpose EV plants to produce gasoline-engine vehicles.

The article cites unnamed sources inside the White House. An unnamed economic advisor calls the move "backward," noting that over 100,000 jobs in the EV sector would be threatened by Trump's new policy, which attempts to undo plans that auto producers have already put in motion. Another source calls it "just a stunt," explaining that "you can't repurpose an EV plant by an order." Autoworkers are furious.

Before you get a chance to process, a longstanding volunteer calls you. Though they've been a steady volunteer, you know most of their work is with the resistance movement. "The resistance has gotten tens of thousands of people to refuse to pay taxes, including several major businesses. We think there's an opportunity for further action to keep the EV industry operating despite the Defense Production Act, but it may get violent and we need help making sure nothing gets out of hand." You nod quietly. You see the potential, but this movement has a history of being…illegal…and a very different kind of work. "We have a plan. Help us?"

YOU'RE CURIOUS WHAT THEY'RE DOING AND TRUST THEY'RE FOR REAL. BUT IT'S A BIG RISK. DO YOU JOIN THEM?

Do not join with other groups, *turn to page 122*
Join with the Resistance to support EV workers, *turn to page 125*

Your friend texts you, "Did you see? Trump's gonna try to stay in power!" You click the link to see what she's talking about. You scan quickly. In Trump's style, he says the quiet part out loud at a midterm rally, "You don't want me going to jail. But the CROOKED COURTS are trying. If I have to, I'll stay President until the courts drop all my cases!"

It goes on to cite unnamed sources inside the White House. One source said Trump was discussing running for a third term — despite the 22nd Amendment, which forbids a President from holding a third term. "Who's gonna stop me?" Another source suggested that Eric Trump might run as a surrogate or perhaps Trump just orders a state of emergency to halt elections for as long as possible. Your heart clenches at any of these possibilities.

Before you get a chance to process, a longstanding volunteer calls you. Though they've been a steady volunteer, you know most of their work is with the Paperclip Movement. "We've got millions wearing paperclips to show we won't obey. But it's time to escalate and really flex our power. We've already used your values in the Convention, but we're promoting a big action where we want you to come out and say you will act on that Convention and get all of your participants — city workers, police, and others — to refuse to obey any acts to prevent a fair and free election." You nod quietly. You understand the logic. But this will be seen as a violation by many members of the Convention, who did not sign up for this. This is a huge ask and very risky. "Trump can't stay in power if we show that we're not going along with this. Help us?"

YOU SEE WHAT THEY'RE DOING AND TRUST THEY'RE FOR REAL. BUT IT'S A BIG RISK. DO YOU JOIN THEM?

Do not join with other groups, *turn to page 122*
Join with the Paperclip resistance movement, *turn to page 126*

Your friend texts you, "Did you see? Trump's announced he's ordering electric vehicle plants to shut down?!" You click the link to see what she's talking about and scan the article quickly. You vaguely remember that when talking about electric vehicles (EVs), Trump promised a "bloodbath" if his opponent was elected. Trump's base has soured on EVs, seeing them as part of the "woke agenda." Trump has now invoked the Defense Production Act to repurpose EV plants to produce gasoline-engine vehicles.

The article cites unnamed sources inside the White House. An unnamed economic advisor calls the move "backward," noting that over 100,000 jobs in the EV sector would be threatened by Trump's new policy, which attempts to undo plans that auto producers have already put in motion. Another source calls it "just a stunt," explaining that "you can't repurpose an EV plant by an order." Autoworkers are furious.

Before you get a chance to process, a longstanding volunteer calls you. Though they've been a steady volunteer, you know most of their work is with the resistance movement. "The Resistance has gotten tens of thousands of people to refuse to pay taxes, including several major businesses. We think there's an opportunity for further action to keep the EV industry operating despite the Defense Production Act — but it may be a prolonged action and we'd need your network to help feed people who might end up… uhm… occupying the factories…" You nod quietly. You see the potential, but this movement has a history of being … illegal… and a very different kind of work. "We have a plan. Help us?"

YOU'RE CURIOUS WHAT THEY'RE DOING AND TRUST THEY'RE FOR REAL. BUT IT'S A BIG RISK. DO YOU JOIN THEM?

Do not join with other groups, *turn to page 122*

Join with the Resistance to support EV workers, *turn to page 125*

Your friend texts you, "Did you see? Trump's gonna try to stay in power!" You click the link to see what she's talking about. You scan quickly. In Trump's style, he says the quiet part out loud at a midterm rally, "You don't want me going to jail. But the CROOKED COURTS are trying. If I have to, I'll stay President until the courts drop all my cases!"

It goes on to cite unnamed sources inside the White House. One source said Trump was discussing running for a third term — despite the 22nd Amendment, which forbids a President from holding a third term. "Who's gonna stop me?" Another source suggested that Eric Trump might run as a surrogate or perhaps Trump just declares a state of emergency to halt elections for as long as possible. Your heart clenches at any of these possibilities.

Before you get a chance to process, a longstanding volunteer calls you. Though they've been a steady volunteer, you know most of their work is with the Paperclip Movement. "We've got millions wearing paperclips to show we won't obey. But it's time to escalate and really flex our power. We're not asking poll workers to break the law. But Trump is going to try to stay in power — and so we need people to follow their oath no matter what he orders. Join us?" This is a huge ask and sounds very risky. "Trump can't stay in power if we show that we're not going along with this. Help us?"

YOU SEE WHAT THEY'RE DOING AND TRUST THEY'RE FOR REAL. BUT IT'S A BIG RISK. DO YOU JOIN THEM?

Do not join with the Paperclip movement, *turn to next page*
Join with the Paperclip movement, *turn to page 126*

You decide not to meet. There's so much to work on. You dive back into your work. It's not until a picnic with your friends that you remember the call. You're with friends on the U.S. Semiquincentennial — July 4, 2026 — marking 250 years since the Declaration of Independence. Someone idly shares, "You hear about the leaders of the Resistance getting arrested and beaten up?" Your ears perk up a little.

With the movement fractured, Trump moves to stay in power. He invokes sketchy emergency orders to "temporarily suspend the 22nd Amendment." Desperate, parts of the disobedience wing of the resistance movement try to mount a one-day strike. Sadly, they aren't able to build a broad coalition. They just never grow fast enough. You realize you could have helped. You were protecting your people and your work — but the situation was too dire.

Trump jams the courts with challenges. By election season, election workers, police, courts, politicians, and the military are all given conflicting orders. Without any clear strategy to resist and no viable alternative, most individuals take the path of least resistance — and put Trump on the ballot. You try to get your groups to take risks, but they aren't ready. He wins a heavily biased election.

During the long years of Trump's regime, a piece of graffiti scrawled on a wall speaks to you. It simply says, "Democracy Requires Risk." You realize that you did fantastic work for the people you impacted — but that you didn't teach them how to resist wrongful orders. So when it came to it, they just weren't ready. You get your people ready. You resolve to be ready to join up with the disobedience wing next time.

The autocrat won this time. But you can try again. In this situation, we're gonna face a moment when groups who are protecting people and defending institutions have to switch up their approach. We'll have to expose our groups to greater risk. We'll have to risk our organizations' existence. We'll have to take great personal risks — otherwise the movement will fail.

Try again — or turn to Closing, page 156

123

One of the leaders from the Strike Committee calls you in tears. "The meeting turned into chaos! People just yelled and…" They take a breath. "It all split apart and now there are four different factions, all with different plans." They stop short of saying you could have made a difference, but they close, "I wish you had been there."

With the movement fractured, Trump moves to stay in power. He invokes sketchy emergency orders to "temporarily suspend the 22nd Amendment." Desperate, parts of the disobedience wing of the resistance movement try to mount a one-day strike. Sadly, they aren't able to build a broad coalition. They just never grow fast enough.

Trump jams the courts with challenges. By election season, election workers, police, courts, politicians, and the military are all given conflicting orders. Without any clear strategy to resist and no viable alternative, most individuals take the path of least resistance — and put Trump on the ballot. You try to get your groups to take risks, but they aren't ready. He wins a heavily biased election.

You know movements are cyclical and there will be another chance to defeat Trump at a later time. Still, you wish you had been able to help see things through.

THE END

The autocrat won this time. But you can try again. In this situation, we're gonna face a moment when groups who are protecting people and defending institutions have to switch up their approach. We'll have to expose our groups to greater risk. We'll have to risk our organizations' existence. We'll have to take great personal risks — otherwise the movement will fail.

Try again — or turn to Closing, page 156

You arrive at a meeting packed with a wide range of different groups, including poll workers and others at the election's front lines. Leaders from the mainstream Constitutional Convention come with an updated Defector's Pledge after results from the 900+ cities that participated in their local conventions. Even some whistleblowers hidden through the Underground Railroad arrive. Fundraising committees come with promises of millions of dollars for a strike fund.

The sense of urgency in the meeting is hot. Whistleblowers confirm rumors that Trump is trying to stay in power for a third term. Colleges have already exploded into walkouts — some violent, often egged on by extremists. In six states, Republican governors sent in the National Guard to quell protests. Using that pretext, the governors of Texas and Florida announce that due to the ongoing "state of emergency," they will be unable to hold elections as planned.

Members of the Strike Committee lead the proceedings, "It is time we escalate into full noncooperation. We need to prepare for ongoing strikes — full disobedience across every sector of society — to insist on having free and fair elections." Nobody disagrees with the need, but disagreement rages about the tactics, the timing, and the methods.

In a country as big as the U.S., and where only 10% of workers are unionized, a full general strike is very difficult. Some grounded facilitation helps hold the meeting together as people come from very different walks of life and inclinations. In the end, it's decided that rolling strikes will commence in two weeks. Rolling strikes allow multiple targets in rapid succession and coordination without day-to-day agreement. Some workplaces shut down for an hour while others stay dark for a week. The demand: free and fair elections.

THE ANNOUNCEMENT OF ROLLING STRIKES IS MADE PUBLICLY. WHAT DOES TRUMP DO?

Trump declares a national state of emergency to delay elections, *turn to page 137*

The Supreme Court orders elections to be held, *turn to page 138*

Trump orders states to carry out elections, but tries to steal them, *turn to page 135*

You arrive at a meeting packed with a wide range of groups, including citizen scientists sending their info to the EPA, multiple national unions and mutual aid groups, people organizing veteran families, members of the Tax Resistance Movement, and leaders of the United Auto Workers (UAW).

Everyone quiets as a leader in the Tax Resistance Movement who is facing 10 years of prison time stands up. "We've all seen how Trump is threatening to shut down EV plants. His order is anti-Constitution. It's anti-environment. It's anti-union and anti-business. It works against the livelihoods of our brothers and sisters in the EV industry. But it provides us an opportunity because it's very much an overreach. He's gotten too cocky and thinks he can get away with anything."

A strategic plan unfolds: The movement is going to shift intense resources to counter Trump's overreach. Some groups don't have direct connections to the issue — but they can see that when an autocratic leader overreaches, it is time to pounce. UAW plans occupy the EV factories — and keep them running despite Trump's order to shut them down. You agree to drive to Michigan plants and provide some support to the occupying workers.

THIS IS A DIRECT CHALLENGE TO TRUMP'S ORDERS. WHAT DOES HE DO IN RESPONSE?

Trump orders the military and police to get workers out, *turn to page 130*
Trump makes wild statements — but doesn't do anything more, *turn to page 131*
Trump tries to change the narrative, *turn to page 132*

You arrive at a meeting packed with a wide range of different groups, including poll workers and others at the election's front lines. Leaders from the mainstream Constitutional Convention come with an updated Defector's Pledge after results from the 900+ cities that participated in their local conventions.

You watch a member of the Paperclip Movement lead the meeting. "Tens of thousands have signed a pledge to resist any orders that go against the Constitution. Now, with Trump saying he wants to stay in power, it's time to act decisively. Eric Trump all but admits he's running 'in name only.' We need to focus our energy on free and fair elections."

You see some unhappy faces. Not everyone thinks this will work. Others are frustrated that the movement is "leaving out other issues." But you see the wisdom. Election workers report that Trump is trying to implement voter restrictions and undermine the process to make it stealable. Direct action is going to be needed. Election workers are going to have to resist orders — especially as Trump is threatening to use the National Guard to "ensure the election is fair."

The meeting concludes with a game plan: Election insiders will go "all in" to support a free and fair election — no matter what orders are made — and the rebel wing of the movement will hold a series of protests up to and after election day.

THE ANNOUNCEMENT OF THESE PLANS IS MADE PUBLICLY. WHAT DOES TRUMP DO?

Trump declares a national state of emergency to delay elections, *turn to page 134*
Trump attempts to steal the election, *turn to page 136*

You agree to organize a large meeting and identify a range of groups to invite, including the Constitutional Convention movement, fundraising groups, and election workers strained by understaffing.

An urgent text from a friend interrupts your day, "Did you see? Trump's gonna try to stay in power!" You click the link to see what she's talking about. You scan quickly. In Trump's style, he says the quiet part out loud at a midterm rally, "You don't want me going to jail. But the CROOKED COURTS are trying. If I have to, I'll stay president until the courts drop all my cases!"

The article goes on to cite unnamed sources inside the White House. One source says Trump is discussing running for a third term — despite the 22nd Amendment, which forbids a president from holding a third term. "Who's gonna stop me?" Another source suggests that Eric Trump might run as a surrogate, or perhaps Trump will just declare a state of emergency to halt elections for as long as possible. Your heart clenches at any of these possibilities.

You realize this upcoming meeting might be the opportunity you need to adjust tactics. The Paperclip Movement could go all-in on the issue of fair elections, making this their major focus. Other voices say this is unwise — the movement needs to stay diverse and respond to the many, many issues Trump's presidency is raising.

YOU SENSE THIS IS A BIG DECISION, WHAT DO YOU DO?

Ditch the large gathering — stay with your own people, *turn to page 108*
Focus the strategy on the election, *turn to page 126*
Keep the strategy as broad as possible, *turn to page 133*

You agree to organize a large meeting and identify a range of groups to invite, including the mutual aid movement and organized veteran families.

A few days before the meeting, an urgent text from a friend interrupts your day, "Did you see? Trump's announced he's ordering electric vehicle plants to shut down?!" You click the link to see what she's talking about and scan the article quickly. You vaguely remember that when talking about electric vehicles (EVs), Trump promised a "bloodbath" if his opponent was elected. Trump's base has soured on EVs, seeing them as part of the "woke agenda." Trump has now invoked the Defense Production Act to repurpose EV plants to produce gasoline-engine vehicles.

The article cites unnamed sources inside the White House. An unnamed economic advisor calls the move "backward," noting that over 100,000 jobs in the EV sector would be threatened by Trump's new policy, which attempts to undo plans that auto producers have already put in motion. Another source calls it "just a stunt," explaining that "you can't repurpose an EV plant by an order." Autoworkers are furious.

This news makes you excited about your upcoming meeting. This attack on EVs might be just the opportunity you need to adjust tactically. You know some people in the autoworkers union. And the Tax Resistance Movement could go "all in" on this issue, making it the major focus of the movement. Other voices within your group say this is unwise — instead, the movement needs to keep building for the next tax season.

YOU SENSE THIS IS A BIG DECISION, WHAT DO YOU DO?

Stay the course with the allies you have, *turn to page 108*
Support EV workers, *turn to page 125*
Stick with with your current strategy, *turn to next page*

You arrive at a meeting packed with a wide range of groups, including poll workers and others at the election's front lines. Fundraising committees come promising money if a meaningful plan is found.

People came because they saw what tax resistance had accomplished: tens of thousands of people and businesses collectively withholding over $500 million from government coffers. Movement leaders say, "And we need to just keep getting bigger — next year we can double this." They lay out a plan…but, based on its reception by the group, you can tell it's not gonna fly.

People complain that another year of Trump feels interminable. "He is securing his position to stay in power for a third term," argues one. "Look what he's doing to the auto industry — he'll kill U.S. auto."

Normally, it's wise to stay focused on your strategy. But you realize this is a special moment. Having a good strategy is key — and knowing when to bend is also important. You think this is one of those moments.

YOU RECONSIDER YOUR CHOICE. MAYBE IT IS TIME TO BACK THE EV INDUSTRY.

Support the EV workers, *turn to page 125*

You spend night after night outside the factory corralling the many newspeople trying to get inside stories, securing food and medicines for people inside the factory, and texting allies around the country to secure their support. Auto companies keep silent, an implicit statement of support to the occupying workers. A CNN interview inside the factory shows workers dutifully caring for the factory equipment and producing U.S.-made electric vehicles.

This creates a bad look for Trump. He looks anti-U.S. jobs. But it's Trump's brand to always double down. He orders the military to force the workers out. "The law is the law. THEY ARE TERRORISTS." He orders all the protests cleared.

Over the next hours, you scramble, calling as many people as you can. People get the memo, and thousands flock to the factory. Throngs of people surround factory entrances.

By the time police and National Guard show up, there's a ring of protestors. The issues are a blurry mix — with some standing for the right to make EVs or cars in general, others demonstrating support for American jobs or unions, and still others there just to defy Trump. The military takes jurisdiction and awaits further orders.

WITH A STANDOFF BETWEEN UNARMED PROTESTORS AND THE MILITARY, WHAT DO YOU DO NEXT?

Recruit the military to join, *turn to page 139*
Organize more people to join the protest, *turn to page 139*
Coordinate national distributed protests across the country, *turn to page 139*

You spend night after night outside the factory corralling the many newspeople trying to get inside stories, securing food and medicines for people inside the factory, and texting allies around the country to secure their support. Auto companies keep silent, an implicit statement of support to the occupying workers. A CNN interview inside the factory shows workers dutifully caring for the factory equipment and producing U.S.-made electric vehicles.

This creates a bad look for Trump. He looks anti-U.S. jobs. Trump won't back down. At 3 am he posts: "WE ARE NOT A BANANA REPUBLIC! FOLLOW THE LAW!!!" And 3:30am: "FIGHT BACK #WEWILLWIN". And at 4 am: "TERRORISTS SHOULD BE SHOT."

The next morning you scramble, calling as many people as you can. People got the memo. Thousands of people flock to the factory, worried about violent counter-protestors. Throngs of people surround factory entrances.

Intending to shut it all down the next morning, police find a ring of determined protestors. The issues are a blurry mix — with some standing for the right to make EVs or cars in general, others demonstrating support for American jobs or unions, and still others there just to defy Trump. Worried about violence, Michigan's governor orders the military to support the police insofar as they can to reduce violence.

WITH A STANDOFF BETWEEN UNARMED PROTESTORS AND THE POLICE, WHAT DO YOU DO NEXT?

Recruit the military to join, *turn to page 139*
Organize more people to join the protest, *turn to page 139*
Coordinate national distributed protests across the country, *turn to page 139*

You spend night after night outside the factory corralling the many newspeople trying to get inside stories, securing food and medicines for people inside the factory, and texting allies around the country to secure their support. Auto companies keep silent, an implicit statement of support to the occupying workers. A CNN interview inside the factory shows workers dutifully caring for the factory equipment and producing U.S.-made electric vehicles.

This creates a bad look for Trump. He looks anti-U.S. jobs. Trump won't back down — so he decides to cut his losses. At 3 am he posts on social media: "MIGRANTS ARE TOSSING BABIES INTO THE RIVER AT THE BORDER. LOOK INTO IT." He tries again: "ILLEGALS KILLED UP TO 200 AMERICANS. THE REAL ISSUE."

The next morning you scramble, calling as many people as you can. People got the memo. Thousands of people flock to the factory. Throngs of people surround factory entrances. Despite some media getting pulled in by Trump, reporters are now embedded in a crowd of thousands — and those images resonate widely.

Police begin setting up barricades around the protestors. The issues are a blurry mix — with some standing against climate change, others demonstrating support for American jobs or unions, and still others there just to defy Trump. Worried about violence, Michigan's governor orders the military to support the police insofar as they can to reduce violence.

WITH A STANDOFF BETWEEN UNARMED PROTESTORS AND THE MILITARY, WHAT DO YOU DO NEXT?

Recruit the military to join, *turn to page 139*
Organize more people to join the protest, *turn to page 139*
Coordinate national distributed protests across the country, *turn to page 139*

You arrive at a meeting packed with a wide range of different groups, including poll workers and others at the election's front lines. Leaders from the mainstream Constitutional Convention come with an updated Defector's Pledge after results from the 900+ cities that participated in their local conventions. Whistleblowers hidden through the Underground Railroad arrive. Fundraising committees come with possibilities of money if a meaningful plan is found.

Members of the Paperclip Movement explain their intention to continue their current strategy — maintaining a broad base with government employees slowing implementation of Trump's orders from the inside. Poll workers ask what they should be doing with the latest news. "Follow your conscience," is the vague reply. You sense that the groups in attendance each have their local focus, but there's no broad, national strategy to avert an impending disaster.

The meeting ends with groups heading in different directions. You can tell this won't work — without a focus, too many people are going to take the path of least resistance.

YOU TALK TO YOUR GROUP — AND URGE THEM TO FOCUS ENERGY ON THE UPCOMING ELECTION.

Focus energy on the election, *turn to page 126*

You feel blindsided when the governors of Texas and Florida announce that due to the ongoing "state of emergency," they will be unable to hold elections as planned. The explosive protests that occur in response to the suspension of elections are cited by the governors as justification for their actions. Hundreds of court cases are filed. It's nonsense.

You are grateful your people have prepared for various scenarios. Thousands fly into Texas and Florida to begin setting up the election infrastructure despite the state's orders. International observers and high-profile right-wing politicians outside of the Trump orbit join. Multiple cities announce they are proceeding with the elections.

The hastily set-up election infrastructure is real. It's solid. And as the movement says, "it's extralegal, extra-Constitutional." You're reminded of the civil rights movement's use of the Mississippi Freedom Democratic Party — a reminder that elections are only as real as we make them.

It's hard to keep track as rumors fly, houses are raided, governors issue condemnations, and the international community condemns the state of emergency. Three more states are considering joining the national state of emergency — which might break your capacity. But when it's clear that Democratic cities in these states will report their election results no matter what, the governors back down and agree to hold elections. They claim "our actions ensured the elections were fair." They order the National Guard "to make sure no riots occur."

AS ELECTION DAY NEARS, YOU WONDER WHICH WAY THINGS WILL SWING.

The election happens, *turn to page 143*

The strike paralyzes large swathes of the country. Ports are periodically closed, and teamsters sometimes refuse to move imports. Wherever Trump travels, roads are blocked and transportation grinds to a standstill. Millions of students walk out of school and attend "strike schools." Some websites shut down, and others are taken down by hackers. Many major retail chains — worried about a cocktail of violence and retribution — preemptively shut down, adding to the effectiveness of the strike. After a particularly rough week, Wall Street trading is suspended for 2 days.

Newspapers report about the economic pain. Trump blames the protestors for causing more chaos. Strike leaders remain firm, saying, "Until we have actionable commitments for a free and fair elections — we hold the line." With so many people off from work, streets are filled with protests daily.

Donald Trump announces, "We will have FAIR ELECTIONS AND WE WILL BEAT THEM." Simultaneously, he introduces a raft of legislation to require national voter IDs and a military presence in Democratic cities to "oversee election security."

Frustrated by the economic pain being inflicted, some urge the group to call off the strikes. But demands have not been achieved. Others urge the Strike Committee to keep going until it achieves actionable results.

SO, WHAT DO YOU DO NEXT?

Continue with the strikes, *turn to page 140*
Call off the strikes, *turn to page 149*

You hear very little about how D.C. insiders from the Paperclip Movement are slowing down Trump. The few that are left move very quietly. But you feel like you see them in action when Trump tries to move a raft of voter restriction bills. He proposes requiring national voter IDs, restricting voting rights for people with criminal convictions, and removing legal protection of voting rights. With the typical chaos of his administration, many of the measures are hastily written and poorly rolled out — congressional and implementation roadblocks seem to appear at every step.

When your phone alerts you that Trump has ordered the National Guard to stand outside of polling places — a clear intimidation tactic — your heart takes a leap. You know what will happen: The court challenges against this will eventually fail. Public sentiment won't like it, but Trump is way past caring about majority public sentiment.

As planned, the resistance movement picks three simultaneous tactics. Some use existing institutions to fight, bringing in international election observers to oversee results and do their own tallies. Others begin organizing election workers to resist restrictions — walking the edge of legality by slow-walking the new measures. And you find yourself in the third wing: public protest.

You attend rambunctious public rallies regularly, encouraging people to "count every vote." The actions look friendly, but the movement is preparing other tactics.

AS ELECTION DAY NEARS, YOU WONDER WHICH WAY THINGS WILL SWING.

The election happens, *turn to page 143*

The strike paralyzes large swathes of the country. Ports are periodically closed, and teamsters sometimes refuse to move imports. Wherever Trump travels, roads are blocked and transportation grinds to a standstill. Millions of students walk out of school and attend "strike schools." Some websites shut down, and others are taken down by hackers. Many major retail chains — worried about a cocktail of violence and retribution — preemptively shut down, adding to the effectiveness of the strike. After a particularly rough week, Wall Street trading is suspended for 2 days.

It's hard to tear yourself away from the news on your phone. Newspapers report about the economic pain. Trump blames the protestors for causing more chaos. Strike leaders remain firm: "Until we have actionable commitments for a free and fair elections — we hold the line." With so many people off from work, streets are filled with protests daily.

Donald Trump calls a state of emergency. "These people are disgusting. They will stop at nothing. This is the DEEP STATE IN ACTION." He rallies people to his side and urges more states to shut down elections "due to the chaos of these woke radicals who called me a dictator from day 1."

Frustrated by the economic pain being inflicted, some urge the group to call off the strikes. But demands have not been achieved. Others urge the Strike Committee to keep going until it achieves actionable results.

SO, WHAT DO YOU DO NEXT?

Continue the strikes, *turn to page 144*
Call off the strikes, *turn to page 142*

The strike paralyzes large swathes of the country. Ports are periodically closed, and teamsters sometimes refuse to move imports. Wherever Trump travels, roads are blocked and transportation grinds to a standstill. Millions of students walk out of school and attend "strike schools." Some websites shut down, and others are taken down by hackers. Many major retail chains — worried about a cocktail of violence and retribution — preemptively shut down, adding to the effectiveness of the strike. After a particularly rough week, Wall Street trading is suspended for 2 days.

Newspapers report about the economic pain. Trump blames the protestors for causing more chaos. Strike leaders remain firm, "Until we have actionable commitments for a free and fair elections — we hold the line." With so many people off from work, streets are filled with protests daily.

The Supreme Court takes up an emergency petition to force the state to carry out elections. Surprising cynics, they return an order relatively quickly, ruling that elections must go forward. Trump lambasts the decision: "PURE POLITICS."

SO, DO THE WAYWARD STATES HONOR THE ORDER?

States honor the orders and affirm elections, *turn to page 145*
States ignore the Supreme Court's orders, *turn to page 146*

You try to do that one thing — but you end up doing them all. You are in a moment of the whirlwind where everything seems to happen at once. You start to call locally to find more people to show up — but the thousands already present begin self-organizing. Mutual aid groups help secure tents and food. That leads you to talking to the police and military to negotiate non-harassment as stuff comes into the factory. Fearful of riots, the military agrees. That leads you to calling across the country to facilitate solidarity actions. It takes very little prodding.

Everyone sees this is a defining fight for Trump — and he's losing. Clearly angry, Trump berates the military about not clearing the protests. "LAWLESSNESS! CHAOS!" But the images on TV only show people calmly tending to everyone's needs. Images loop of workers inside the factory wiping down machines with care. Two automaker CEOs explain that they want to produce EVs — "and we want to do it in the U.S."

You watch in shock as Trump's antics look more and more like tantrums. He's not been well and, as people explain, his autocratic streak cannot be restrained. He orders Congress to impeach the military generals — but is immediately rebuked. He then orders the Proud Boys to "STEP IN AND FIX THIS." This becomes his undoing.

The Proud Boys do descend. The military does not let them get close to the protestors — and after hours of violence, they slink away.

ALONG WITH THE COUNTRY, YOU BRACE FOR WHAT'S NEXT.

Elections are held and Trump loses, *turn to page 148*

Buoyed by Trump's rhetoric, counter-protestors attempt high-profile, targeted violence. They go to actions in major cities and attack protesters with bats. Though fear ripples through the resistance movement, counter-protesters are severely outnumbered and their actions fail to stem the tide of people in the streets. Artists flood the streets with music — to reduce fear — and pieces of art that also serve as physical ways to keep distance from counter-protestors.

The Trump-incited violence backfires. Seeing violent Trump supporters contrasted with the discipline and positivity of the protestors wins over more allies. Reports pour in about how the U.S. economy is losing substantial amounts of money daily from the strikes. Corporate CEOs privately meet with Republican senators to find a resolution; some threaten to take their business out of the country.

Despite the best efforts of funding committees, strike funds are depleted. Mutual aid groups step into some of the breaches. They try to meet the needs of workers, many now without jobs, paychecks, or housing. The work with the veteran families pays off. Retired military generals announce that it's an "unlawful order" to interfere with the outcome of the election.

Major political donors worry that the country could fall off an economic precipice, influencing the Senate to kill all of Trump's attempts to introduce restrictive laws. Following the public death of his bills, a back deal is made: All states allow elections in exchange for ending the strike. With some controversy, the strike is ended — and the states allow elections to happen.

SO, WHAT IS THE RESULT?

Trump fails to steal election, *turn to next page*

The election is held. It is unruly and chaotic. Rules across states vary, and implementation of rules is uneven — some district judges attempt to enact late orders like requiring voter IDs. Others refuse. Election observers refuse to call it a uniformly clean election. Trump tried to steal the election.

But you are proud of your work. The structure of the national Strike Committee is well suited to transform itself to support overwhelming voter turnout. It is broadly trusted by the public even when the opposition spreads rumors to deter voting: A line of voters in Philadelphia has been shot at by passing cars. Militia members are sitting 100 feet from polling stations in downtown Portland. Teams are sent to targeted polling stations to encourage confidence in the election.

After many protests and contested legal fights, the election goes forward. A new slate of political leaders is put into power. The number of incumbents defeated is the highest in generations, with a wave of independents riding on the coattails of the resistance movement's energy. Many newly elected leaders have already given their pledge to abide by the outcome of the democracy-modeled Constitutional Convention, with its sensible recommendations coming from now over 2,000 cities.

The federal reforms happen first. New laws affirm that money is not speech and put an end to gerrymandering. The bill for term limits for all federal leaders barely passes — only passing with a controversial exemption for current senators and house members. There is an end to right-to-work legislation and support for card check neutrality. The changes take place, buoyed by a movement that keeps up regular protests and occasional strikes. You feel proud of your role in all of it.

You managed to push out the autocrat! You did not do it alone. Like in real life, many approaches had to work together to get to this point: defending democratic institutions, supporting a vibrant disobedience wing, protecting individuals being targeted, and building alternative visions beyond just "a return to normal."

Try again — or turn to Closing, page 156

You try to call off the strikes but are almost laughed out of your meetings. "We haven't won anything and there's too much at stake." The group ignores you and you feel a little embarrassed.

Strikes work on the concept of solidarity. You realize the strike has to continue — though you still worry it may not have enough power to win.

SO, WHAT DO YOU DO NOW?

Continue with the strikes, *turn to page 144*

You don't sleep the night of the election. CNN covers the election returns, verifying the official results with a raft of international election observers. The election will come down to just a handful of states, and it will take weeks to count all the votes.

To no one's surprise, just three hours after the polls close, Donald Trump announces "ERIC TRUMP WON! IT'S OVER!" A group of retired election workers delivers a scathing rebuke: "Nobody wins until the votes are counted."

The next weeks stretch into an eternity. With only two states left in play, Trump announces "the results are decided" and openly tells Philadelphia election workers to stop counting. Philadelphians pour into the Convention Center for a dance party "to support the election workers." Philly police make no moves to stop the counting.

You're walking outside when CNN calls the election against the Trumps. You stop in your tracks. For a moment you think it might be over. But Trump tweets again that he's a victor and will refuse to vacate office based on a "RIGGED ELECTION EVEN BIGGER THAN LAST TIME."

IT'S GOING TO BE A CONTEST OF WILLS. WHAT DO YOU DO?

Descend on D.C. "to help him pack his bags", *turn to page 150*
Nothing — let the military sort it out, *turn to page 151*

Buoyed by Trump's rhetoric, counter-protestors attempt high-profile, targeted violence. They go to actions in major cities and attack people with bats. Though fear ripples through the movement, they are severely outnumbered and their actions fail to stem the tide of people in the streets. Artists flood the streets with music — to reduce fear — and pieces of art that also serve as physical ways to keep distance from counter-protestors.

The Trump-incited violence backfires. Seeing violent Trump supporters contrasted with the discipline and positivity of the protestors wins over more allies. Reports pour in about how the U.S. economy is losing substantial amounts of money daily from the strikes. Corporate CEOs privately meet with Republican senators to find a resolution; some threaten to take their business out of the country.

Despite the best efforts of funding committees, strike funds are depleted. Mutual aid groups step into some of the breaches. They try to meet the needs of workers, many now without jobs, paychecks, or housing. Expanding the definition of "strike," election workers vow to carry out the elections anyway. Many hours of volunteer and expert labor goes into making the states' elections happen despite the unlawful orders from the states. When election workers are arrested by police, retired military personnel show up outside jail cells with signs: "A Democracy Needs Election Workers."

Texas breaks first. Under pressure from CEOs and business interests, the governor agrees to a backdoor deal allowing elections in exchange for an end to all strikes in Texas. This is controversial. But, now isolated, Florida soon follows suit. Within hours, strike leaders have confirmed the authenticity of the deal and all strikes are ended.

SO, WHAT NEXT?

A relatively free and fair election is held, *turn to page 147*

Buoyed by Trump's rhetoric, counter-protestors attempt high-profile, targeted violence. They go to actions in major cities and attack people with bats. Though fear ripples through the movement, they are severely outnumbered and their actions fail to stem the tide of people in the streets. Artists flood the streets with music — to reduce fear — and pieces of art that also serve as physical ways to keep distance from counter-protestors.

Election workers prepare to carry out the elections either way — but there is no need. In a coordinated response, Texas and Florida both announce they will carry out elections as required. The strike lasts 12 more hours as the details are ironed out and confirmed.

THE STRIKE ENDS — AND ELECTIONS ARE INDEED CARRIED OUT. WHAT NEXT?

A relatively free and fair election is held, *turn to page 147*

The states completely ignore the Supreme Court's order. This is met by outrage — and for a moment a sense that it's all unwinnable. The Supreme Court has no army to enforce the order and the states claim, "With the ongoing strikes, it's impossible to carry out elections."

Buoyed by Trump's rhetoric, counter-protestors attempt high-profile, targeted violence. They go to actions in major cities and attack people with bats. Though fear ripples through the movement, they are severely outnumbered and their actions fail to stem the tide of people in the streets. Artists flood the streets with music — to reduce fear — and pieces of art that also serve as physical ways to keep distance from counter-protestors.

Reports pour in about how the U.S. economy is losing substantial amounts of money daily from the strikes. Corporate CEOs privately meet with Republican senators to find a resolution; some threaten to take their business out of the country. Expanding the definition of "strike," election workers vow to carry out the elections anyway. Many hours of volunteer and expert labor goes into making the states' elections happen despite the unlawful orders from the states. When election workers are arrested by police, retired military personnel show up outside jail cells with signs: "A Democracy Needs Election Workers."

The economic pain is unbearable. Texas breaks first. Under pressure from CEOs and business interests, the governor agrees to a backdoor deal allowing elections in exchange for an end to all strikes in Texas. This is controversial. But, now isolated, Florida soon follows suit. Within hours, strike leaders have confirmed the authenticity of the deal and all strikes are ended.

THE STRIKE ENDS — AND ELECTIONS ARE INDEED CARRIED OUT. WHAT NEXT?

A relatively free and fair election is held, *turn to next page*

Over the next months, your mood swings from giddy to despairing. Elections are held. Reports of violence spike. A new slate of political leaders is put into power. The number of incumbents defeated is the highest in generations. Vows of vengeance from Trump supporters continue. But many new officials ride in on the coattails of the resistance movement and are elected having made democracy-minded promises.

Your movement didn't just win elections — they've won pledges to abide by the outcomes of the deep democracy-modeled Constitutional Convention. Its sensible recommendations come from now over 2,000 cities.

The federal reforms happen first. New laws affirm that money is not speech and put an end to gerrymandering. The bill for term limits for all federal leaders barely passes — only passing with a controversial exemption for current senators and house members. There is an end to right-to-work legislation and support for card check neutrality.

The changes take place, buoyed by a movement that keeps up regular protests and occasional strikes. You continue your work, aware of much more to do. And you feel proud of your role in all of it.

THE END

You managed to push out the autocrat! You did not do it alone. Like in real life, many approaches had to work together to get to this point: defending democratic institutions, supporting a vibrant disobedience wing, protecting individuals being targeted, and building alternative visions beyond just "a return to normal."

Try again — or turn to Closing, page 156

You had seen the fractures. Trump had embarrassed nearly all elite Republican leaders. He'd sicced mobs against some of them. He had strong-armed others. So when he started looking like a loser, they bailed. But you were still shocked when news came across your phone that his own Justice Department was announcing an investigation into his "possibly calling for an insurrection."

You read an article by a theoretician named Timur Kuran talking about "unanticipated revolution" — where a political leader who seems to have full support suddenly has it evaporate. Given Trump's near absolute dominance of the Republican Party, you don't expect what follows.

Trump fires a dozen Justice Department officials until he finds one willing to dismiss the case against him. But even then he looks weaker. Most of the 2028 presidential hopefuls agree that the case should be reopened if they win office. Every Trump maneuver to extend his power through controlling the elections fails. He has lost his juice.

You are not surprised when Trump loses in 2028. He claims election fraud — but even his own party only pays lip service to that theory. The insurrection case is reinstated. You know all this only came about because of a vibrant, risk-taking movement. You continue your work, aware there is much more to do. And you feel proud of your role in all of it.

THE END

You managed to push out the autocrat! You did not do it alone. Like in real life, many approaches had to work together to get to this point: defending democratic institutions, supporting a vibrant disobedience wing, protecting individuals being targeted, and building alternative visions beyond just "a return to normal."

Try again — or turn to Closing, page 156

You try to call off the strikes but are almost laughed out of your meetings. "We haven't won anything and there's too much at stake." The group ignores you and you feel a little embarrassed.

Strikes work on the concept of solidarity. You realize the strike has to continue — though you still worry it may not have enough power to win.

SO, WHAT DO YOU DO NOW?

Continue with the strikes, *turn to page 140*

Swarms of people head to D.C. to "help Trump pack his bags." Unlike the last time Trump tried to stay in power, the resistance movement is clear about calling it a coup and what the steps are to stop a coup. Hundreds of thousands of people stay in D.C. to "see him out." All day, Trump hides in the White House trying to coordinate a response.

History rides on some really close calls. According to international observers, the official results were tainted by hundreds of local polling places being manipulated. Despite the manipulation, Trump lost by narrow margins in key states. And when a small bomb went off and injured 20 anti-Trump protestors in D.C., public opinion swung against Trump. But it didn't displace him. The movement vows to peaceably, but forcibly, escort him out.

Inauguration day brings vicious counter-protests. You feel history could have gone either way. But the resistance movement has given the military all the rationale they need to escort Trump out of office. When confronted with that possibility, Trump very reluctantly walks out of the White House and heads home to Mar-a-Lago.

A new president takes over a battered, bruised nation. Trump is eventually charged with insurrection, but dies before the trial. The Constitutional Convention is able to undo many of his worst measures and tighten up existing laws to avoid such chaotic orders in the future. The movement averted another coup — but just by the skin of its teeth. You feel proud of everything you did to help make this happen.

THE END

You managed to push out the autocrat! You did not do it alone. Like in real life, many approaches had to work together to get to this point: defending democratic institutions, supporting a vibrant disobedience wing, protecting individuals being targeted, and building alternative visions beyond just "a return to normal."

Try again — or turn to Closing, page 156

Nobody goes to D.C. to help Trump pack his bags. Instead, Trump supporters swarm the U.S. Capitol building. Their numbers aren't as large as they were at the insurrection on January 6, 2021 — but their presence is a deterrent to any massive anti-Trump protests. A few antifa groups show up and instigate violent confrontations with the Trump supporters. You realize right away that it was a strategic mistake to not go to D.C.

When Trump refuses to leave office, the military is confronted with a painful choice: undermine peaceful transfer of power or follow their current commander's orders. They choose what feels like the easier course, and Trump stays in the White House.

After this, Army generals are permanently seen as political forces — deciders of future elections. Anyone seeking the office of president now has to have secret meetings with military elites to seek their approval. This undermines the government. You wish pro-democracy people had gone into the street to lead the way. You regret your decision and hope that if elections are held in the future, you'll be able to control the outcome better.

THE END

You did not push out the autocrat. Your reliance on the military backfired. They are in a tough position and needed constant active public support to give cover. Public pressure in the form of marches and protest and mass displays of opposition are necessary ingredients.

Try again — or turn to Closing, page 156

Police Arrest Liz Cheney

At 6:34 am this morning, former U.S. Representative Liz Cheney was arrested at her home in Jackson Hole, Wyoming. Trump had ordered the Justice Department to investigate her and all members of the House Select Committee on the January 6th Attack. The Justice Department has said it does not yet find evidence of wrongdoing in the other cases, "but we are still looking."

Liz Cheney's lawyers refute the "bizarre charges," calling them "fully unsubstantiated accusations of terrorism and incitement that should never have been brought." Liz Cheney's arrest has sparked public outrage, with sporadic protests breaking out since the news. Based on the charges, she faces a sentence of up to 20 years in prison. A Trump spokesperson only said, "Justice is being done."

A spokesperson for a group that has been advocating tax resistance to stop Donald Trump said, "This is clearly political vengeance. Since this news, over 5,000 new people have signed saying they will refuse to pay their taxes to such a blatantly repressive government." This resistance has shocked many in the Republican establishment. Private signs of Republican weariness with Trump seem to be growing. "I didn't think this would happen, I really didn't," said Senator Lindsey Graham, clearly surprised. Nonetheless, Graham refused to condemn the arrest.

Cheney is the most well known among dozens of political prisoners who have been arrested after challenging Trump. A network calling themselves the "Underground Railroad" claims more than 2,000 whistleblowers and other vulnerable people have fled persecution through their network, including several staff members of the Select Committee on the January 6th Attack.

Trump's Health Department Declares "Men Are Men" Policy

Under new guidelines from the Trump administration, the Department of Health and Human Services has announced a "men are men" policy. In a memo that reads more like a policy paper, health providers are ordered to "direct any people with gender dysphoria into appropriate therapy." This comes as the Trump administration has introduced a bill that will ban gender-affirming care for minors nationwide.

The bill and memo both faced swift backlash. The American Medical Association and the American Academy of Pediatrics have both come out against the bill: "There is no basis for denying care." A spokesperson for the Paperclip Movement — a group that has been organizing resistance against what they call "anti-constitutional" Trump policies — says it has already organized dozens of hospitals in several states to refuse to abide by these rules.

The bill appears unlikely to pass in Congress. But it comes as Republican states have restricted trans rights. Ten states have introduced new legislation to curtail access to gender-affirming care for minors. Since Trump's first year in office, five states have passed other bills targeting the trans community's participation in school sports that aligns with their gender identity and restricting books and sex education materials that affirm trans identities.

Trans-led mutual aid networks have popped up across the country to replace these materials and, in some cases, even secretly smuggle them back into schools. One spokesperson said, "They can try to ban us. They can try to get rid of our health care. They can try to deny us housing, credit, and public accommodations. They can try to shame us. They can try all they want to erase us, but at some point, they will realize the trans community is never going away."

Racial Hate Crimes Rise — Prosecutions Down

A federal report from the Justice Department notes that racial hate crimes have gone up by 85% since the start of Trump's term, even while their prosecutions went down by 34%. "This reflects administration priorities," says a spokesperson, who listed Trump talking points about stopping crime, even though experts say that overall, crime rates have flatlined.

Many point to Trump's dismantling of "disparate-impact theory," which allowed the government to stop policies that disproportionately affect a marginalized group. "This has allowed LGBTQ tenants to get kicked out on the flimsiest of pretexts and Black business owners to be denied bank loans that white business owners get," said one expert. An independent report suggested within the first year of this change, hundreds of millions of dollars have been lost by Black businesses due to racial bias.

In response, the NAACP urged its members to "resist national policy that seeks to destroy our communities." It has recently joined a national Strike Committee, which plans to organize various wildcat strikes unless its list of demands are met — which include a vow for President Trump to "affirm free and fair elections." A Trump spokesperson calls these efforts "a joke."

A national fundraising network has pledged to plow more money into local prosecutions "to make up for the lack of federal Justice Department spending." They acknowledge it is very difficult to take up federal racial-bias cases without active support from the Justice Department. Instead, they primarily lean on local and state human rights commissions.

Trump Controls Purse Strings to Enforce Comstock Act

Donald Trump tried a new escalation to pass the "Comstock Act 2.0", named after a long-dormant 19th-century law. In clear horse trading, he's refusing to fund programs Congress has earmarked in its budget until they pass laws that strengthen the Comstock Act. The Comstock Act was originally passed in 1873. It bans mailing "obscene, lewd, lascivious, indecent, filthy or vile articles," including abortion-inducing medications. Trump is proposing an even more expansive bill.

Up until now, lower courts have been wary of setting public policy on abortion and have denied attempts to expand the Comstock Act to include drugs used in abortion procedures. To force Congress's hand, Trump claims the Impoundment Control Act does not apply to him. The Impoundment Control Act was enacted in 1974 after President Nixon refused to spend money on projects Congress had authorized. Without it, the President would effectively gain the right to ignore congressional budgets and spend the federal budget completely at his own discretion.

The moves caused private resistance among Republicans in Washington. "Trump can't help himself — he just wants power," said one Republican senator, who noted that he agrees with Trump on defunding liberal priorities like the EPA and election security. But he railed against "too much Presidential authority." Experts say that Trump's maneuver won't stand up in court — but they note that it's likely that many of Congress's priorities will be unfunded until the courts step in. Trump has targeted EPA, election security, and other liberal priorities.

Democrats introduced an alternative bill, which has little chance of passing, that would fully fund departments like the EPA to levels during the Biden administration. "Citizen scientists are volunteering doing the work of EPA because Trump's moving to completely defund it. We've got people doing fundraisers for our election systems and roads and Trump is just finding new ways to take it all away."

Trump Proposes Outlawing Electric Vehicles

After landing in D.C. from a trip to China, Trump declared "weak EV trucks and cars should be outlawed." The statement surprised his aides, who said this was "an unplanned announcement." Electric vehicles (EVs), including cars and trucks, run on rechargeable batteries instead of carbon-producing combustion engines. Trump has floated rescinding parts of Biden's Inflation Reduction Act that support building the network of EV charging stations and subsidizing EVs.

Automakers have largely stayed silent. But one expert who wished to remain anonymous said China is now leading the "EV arms race, and this will only make it worse." Trump does not appear to have the votes to undercut the EV industry entirely. But by creating a hostile environment, production of U.S.-made EVs has slowed, while the import of Chinese EVs has grown.

Environmental groups made a joint statement attacking Trump's climate policy. "As climate-change-fueled fires tear through the Southwest and floods cover the Northeast, Trump is doubling down on the policies that created this problem." They note that EVs are only a small part of what they call "solutions to the climate problem." "We should be talking about mass transit, about a just transition out of the fossil fuel era."

The head of the United Auto Workers (UAW) could not be reached for comment, but a UAW spokesperson said, "If Trump loves American jobs, he shouldn't threaten them." A Trump spokesperson responded, "We will only Make America Great Again with what makes our country great and safe: guns, gas trucks, and good old American values."

ICE Shoots 3 in Standoff with Immigrants

What started as a typical Immigration and Customs Enforcement (ICE) raid turned deadly after a standoff in San Diego. The raid was carried out under Trump's "Operation Clean Up," which shut off Title 42 to end asylum for immigrants, reinstated family separations on the border, and announced a plan for the sweeping mass deportation of undocumented immigrants. "We heard about a house full of illegals, and we went to remove them," said an ICE official.

Neighbors who found out about the raid allegedly stood outside the apartment and confronted ICE. San Diego County has a "sanctuary" policy against police colla-boration with ICE. ICE convinced the Texas governor to order the Texas Army National Guard across the border and into California. More neighbors came through the night — 200 people in all. One immigrant in the house spoke through a translator, "I've lived here for 26 years. I pay my taxes and have raised three kids here. I'm a friend, not a combatant."

Late in the night, an unidentified agent scuffled with neighbors before pulling out their firearm and firing at least six times. Three people were injured and are expected to recover. Police arrived and successfully ordered ICE and the National Guard away. The crowd dispersed. Neighbors report the immigrants are now finding a safe new home via the Underground Railroad.

No arrests have been made. Stephen Miller, the acting head of ICE, defended his policy. "A nation without borders is not a nation." Through a network of veteran families, several retired Army generals urged the National Guard not to be politicized this way. "We are not Immigration Enforcement. We protect the American population to live in safety." A civic group who had plans around the corner is calling for a national Constitutional Convention and said, "This is a tragedy. We need honest debates — neighbors shouldn't need to risk their lives when policies are so out of step with the public wishes." The group is organizing towns across the country to host conventions to debate changes to the Constitution, including changing our immigration policies. The new date for their convention is next week.

READING THE NEWS IS SCARY, BUT GIVES YOU A BETTER SENSE OF WHAT IS HAPPENING. YOU FEEL BETTER PREPARED.

Return to your bookmarked page. If you lost it, find your path here based on what you were organizing:

Mutual aid society, *turn to page 46*

Joint emergency fundraising, *turn to page 47*

The Underground Railroad, *turn to page 48*

Cultural grounding for the movement, *turn to page 53*

Constitutional Convention, *turn to page 55*

Veteran families, *turn to page 56*

Citizen scientists to help the EPA, *turn to page 57*

To protect the election, *turn to page 58*

The Paperclip Movement, *turn to page 75*

National Strikes, *turn to page 83*

Tax Resistance Movement, *turn to page 91*

CLOSING

If I were sitting next to you, I'd want to ask you what you thought and saw from this experience. I'd be curious what scared you, what made you feel more prepared, and how you plan to handle your emotional journey no matter what happens. Likely you'd have other scenarios that would pop into your head and I'd be interested to hear what you think might happen.

No, this isn't trying to be a crystal ball. Yes, you're probably right some things would happen differently. Yes, it's true the make-up of Congress would matter a lot. Sure, that part is unlikely to happen like that …

I would want to remind you that very little of Trump's actions in this adventure did I make up. It largely comes from his words. (At WhatIfTrumpWins.org you can see footnotes connected to many of his major moves.) His friends at Project 2025 have published 900-pages of their terrifying plans.

But the goal of this adventure is to pivot away from just what might Trump do — and towards the question: *What will you do?*

There are many, many roles in social resistance. If any version of these events comes to be, there will be an abundant number of needs. You will be needed. This adventure explores a couple major approaches. Two approaches I urge against are **staying purely in a reactive mode** and **actions that only express opinions** — posting on social media or marching in the street. These can grow our confidence, but *alone* they build no political power to change the course of things. Please don't get me wrong — these can be helpful tactics in the mix. But a resistance movement that's too reliant on these approaches will be quickly devastated.

If you replay the adventure, you'll find four approaches that do help:
- Folks who defend existing institutions
- Folks who protect folks who are being targeted
- Folks who envision and create alternative institutions
- Folks who engage in strategic civil disobedience

Each group has gifts and challenges (and in reality may not be distinct at all). The first two approaches — **defend existing institutions** and **protect folks who are targeted** — are gifted helpers. They want to protect and defend. Thus they want to avoid conflict and keep people from being targeted. However, in an autocratic environment, that cannot be guaranteed. In fact, in order for the movement to win there will be moments where folks will have to do a difficult thing: cast aside their conflict aversion and *actively step into risk*.

At certain stages and big moments, they'll have to join the **strategic disobedience** wings. That wing can be bold, dramatic, and to be effective it needs to understand the art of timing. Calling for civil disobedience too early exposes weaknesses. They have to stay in touch with moderate groups to assess for the right moment. They have to show that disobedience can, to a degree, gain ground and protect people. If other strategies don't stop an autocrat (and once in office those approaches rarely do), this wing calls everyone to escalated action.

All the while there are folks who **envision and create alternative institutions.** They help the fight be more than just "preserving democracy." Autocracy looks attractive because the old model of so-called democracy was deficient. This group holds vision, high-values, and a potent mix of wild idealism and practical demonstrations of a better system.

The reality is few of us think we can "stop Trump." We vote. Angst. And then what? Sadly, our teachers and media do us no favors in terms of teaching the strategies for resistance. Media might tell you things are bad — but rare is the article that helps you answer "what can I do?"

I hope this adventure supports you, even a little, to envision yourself helping neighbors seeking political shelter — fundraising for your local election protection organizations — or, yes, joining and even leading wildcat strikes.

If any of these things come to pass, we will all have a role to play. Hopefully you're a little more prepared to play it.

If you want more, we have resources on our website: WhatIfTrumpWins.org. We have articles about these different approaches, scenario tools you can lead with your local groups, and interviews with people who have fought autocracies.

We got this.

Daniel Hunter (May 2024)

ABOUT THE CONTRIBUTORS

Daniel Hunter, author

In 2004, Daniel co-founded Choose Democracy to train tens of thousands about what to do in case of a Trump coup. He has trained pro-democracy movements in Burma/Myanmar, Thailand, India, and many other places.

Daniel has written multiple books: *Building a Movement to End the New Jim Crow*, *Climate Resistance Handbook*, and *Strategy and Soul* — a thrilling personal story about community organizing and direct action.

With over three decades of activist training experience, his training tools are used across the globe for helping people fight for a better, more democratic world.

Elizabeth Beier, artist

Elizabeth Beier is a freelance illustrator, graphic facilitator and painter. Over a diverse career she often returns to the meeting point between art, writing, and activism. From 2016-2018 she authored and illustrated political comics for *The Lily,* a feminist project within *The Washington Post*.

Her first published book, *The Big Book of Bisexual Trials and Errors,* was named by Advocate.com as one of the best LGBT graphic novels of 2017. She first became involved with Choose Democracy in 2020 by creating animations that illustrated tactics to stop a coup. Since 2023 Beier has contracted with the group Illustrating Progress to provide storytelling and artwork for social justice causes.

CHOOSE ☑ DEMOCRACY

The year was 2020. We were in the middle of a pandemic, heightened police violence, multiple uprisings, massive wildfires, and a federal election. **Months before the election, President Donald Trump warned us that he would reject unfavorable election results.**

Many people brushed it off. *We didn't.* The great sage Maya Angelou warned us, "When someone shows you who they are, believe them the first time." We believed and starting as an all-volunteer team created Choose Democracy. We shared lessons evidence-based lessons about stopping a coup from movements from around the world. We trained tens of thousands on what to do if there was an election-related power grab — a coup — across the political spectrum.

We continue to house resources on stopping coups on the web: **ChooseDemocracy.us**

In 2024, we reformed again to shared time-tested strategy from people who have fought against autocratic uprisings. We freely share all our resources, interviews, articles, and training materials at:

WhatIfTrumpWins.org

Made in the USA
Monee, IL
06 November 2024

69501742R00090